VOICES

FROM THE MID-SOUTH

Newspaper Columns and Con...

& GUIDELINES FOR WRITI...

BOOK DESIGN BY JEAN STRONG

PRAIRIE ALMANAC PUBLISHER
PO Box 1312
Bentonville, AR 72712-1312

Printed and bound by Morris Publishing, 3212 E. Hwy 30, PO Box 2110, Kearney, NE 68847 (800-650-7888)
First printing August 2002

ISBN: 09626572-4-7
Library of Congress Control Number: 2001097766

SPECIAL THANKS

To Anita French Creech and **Cynthia Haseloff** for permitting the use of their work in this book of columns and comments.
To friends who reviewed *VOICES* prior to publication,
and to those who offer book signings in Northwest Arkansas.

To Steve Semken, Ice Cube Press / Book Design & Production
for production assistance. 205 N. Front, North Liberty, Iowa 52317.
[E-mail icecube@inav.net, phone 319-626-2055, http://soli.inav.net/~icecube

Credits

The original publishers – The Cedar Rapids Gazette, The Morning News, and Community Publishers, Inc. (CPI) – have graciously granted permission to reprint the columns that appeared first in the their papers.

The Cedar Rapids Gazette, Cedar Rapids, Iowa

The Morning News
Springdale, Rogers, Fayetteville, Bentonville

The Benton County Daily Record
Bentonville and Benton County (CPI)
(Delivered since August 2000 as wraparound
for the *Arkansas Democrat-Gazette*, Northwest Edition)

The Weekly Vista, Bella Vista (CPI)

The Herald-Democrat, Siloam Springs (CPI)
(Formerly *The News Leader*)

Reference Books FOR TRIBUTE AND COMMENTS

THE STORY OF WINSLOW'S MAUD DUNCAN
Robert G. Winn
Sponsored by the Bank of Fayetteville with the Washington County Historical Society, 1992
Permission granted by Shiloh Museum of Ozark History
Caretaker of R.G. Winn estate records

ROBERTA A MOST REMARKABLE FULBRIGHT
Dorothy D. Stuck & Nan Snow
University of Arkansas Press, 1997
Permission granted to reprint quotes by and about Roberta Fulbright

CONTENTS

~ INTRODUCTION ~

Newspapers in Our "Little Bit of Wonderful"

TWO competing dailies serve fortunate newspaper readers in beautiful Northwest Arkansas. One is *The Benton County Daily Record*, Bentonville—an edition since August 2000 of the state's *Arkansas Democrat-Gazette.* The other is *The Morning News*, Springdale (Stephens Media Group).

The Daily Record and *The Morning News* first published most of the columns featured in VOICES FROM THE MID-SOUTH. The largest cities in "our" Northwest Arkansas are Fayetteville, Springdale, Rogers and Bentonville. Fayetteville and Bentonville are county seats. Both news organizations vie for dominance in the cities, small towns and rural areas of the region.

"The region continues to offer opportunities for future columnists who, by the way, must pay their dues as reporters before assuming the columnist mantle with any of the local newspapers," says Jim Morriss, *Morning News* executive editor.

"Topics abound. The region is in transition, with a metropolitan lifestyle evolving from a totally rural environment, and the ongoing efforts to achieve a balance between the two is fertile ground for reporting and commentary," Morris added.

"The best material for community newspaper columns generally isn't a weighty national subject," says Kent Marts, *Daily Record* editor. "The best material covers matters that are often close to the hearts of the writers."

The unusual competitive newspaper situation here in the 21st century is evaluated in an informative book masterminded by veteran editor-in-chief Gene Roberts. *Leaving Readers Behind, The Age of Corporate Newspapering* (University of Arkansas Press 2001) features a series of reports by nine writers who scrutinized the American newspaper industry over a two-year period. They found that independent newspapers everywhere are an "endangered species," that "the typical daily is mediocre" and remind us that the "two major cost centers of newspapering are people and paper."

Benton and Washington counties are in one of the most competitive newspaper markets in America, according to the report by Jack Bass. He adds: "It does seem to suggest that preserving editorial competition can improve newspaper quality and provide for a better-informed citizenry." A former weekly newspaper publisher, Bass is a professor of humanities with six books to his credit.

The *Arkansas Democrat-Gazette* (Little Rock) prints its Northwest Edition at Lowell. Its parent organization, WEHCO Media, also owns papers at Hot Springs, El Dorado and Texarkana with a total circulation of about 234,000.

Stephens Media Group owns *The Morning News* (37,000 circulation) and dailies at Fort Smith and Pine Bluff for a total circulation of just over 95,000. *The Morning News* serves four counties—Washington, Benton, Carroll and Madison. Stephens also owns three weeklies at Farmington, Prairie Grove and Lincoln in Washington County.

In Benton County smaller communities include Bella Vista, Cave Springs and Centerton, Decatur, Garfield, Gateway, Gentry and Gravette, Highfill which is the locale of the Northwest Regional Airport (XNA) and Hiwasse, Lowell and Pea Ridge, Siloam Springs and Sulphur Springs. The airport, created in the 1990s, contributes to the rapid population growth with the resulting strain on infrastructure in the town, city and county governments.

In Washington County other communities include Cincinnati, Elkins and Elm Springs, Greenland and Goshen and Tonitown.

In another chapter titled "The Selling of Small-Town America," Mary Walton reports "a frenzy of selling" amid all daily newspapers between January 1994 and July 2000. Among the nation's 1,483 dailies, no less than 719 transactions took place during that six-year period. Some papers changed ownership "two, three or even four times," she said. Walton is a former newspaper reporter who writes for magazines and has authored four books.

The Northwest Arkansas Times in Fayetteville (published by Roberta Fulbright from 1923 to 1952) was among the papers that changed hands twice and accounts for two of twelve transactions in Arkansas during the period.

Community Publishers, Inc. of Bentonville, purchased the *Times* in 1999 as its circulation approached 14,000. The *Times*, like its sister publication, *The Benton County Daily Record*, is delivered as a wraparound local edition of the Northwest Edition of the *Arkansas Democrat-Gazette*. The Northwest Edition goes to a 12-county area in Northwest Arkansas while the *Times* serves Washington County and the *Record* serves Benton County. Combined circulation for CPI's Benton and Washington county dailies is estimated at 32,500, based on the 2001 Gale Directory of Publications, 135th edition.

Community Publishers, Inc. also owns the *Harrison Daily Times* (Boone County) and weekly newspapers in Bella Vista, Decatur, Gentry, Gravette, Rogers, Pea Ridge and Siloam Springs in Benton County; and Elkins in Washington County. Both CPI and *The Morning News* maintain a strong presence in Northwest Arkansas.

Of her editor, Roberta Fulbright wrote:

*"Lessie Read may have faults, but they are **not**
lack of honesty, courage or energy."*

TRIBUTE TO COLUMNISTS
IN NW ARKANSAS

VOICES FROM THE MID-SOUTH applauds all columnists for sharing experiences and insights with readers of community and daily newspapers—especially those in 'our little bit of wonderful' that is Northwest Arkansas, sharing borders with Missouri to the north and Oklahoma to the west.

You will get to know

Anita French Creech
Business writer

Cynthia Haseloff
Novelist

Jean Strong
Retired journalist

as you read their Columns and Comments.

The last chapter outlines an informal program to help develop and hone your own writing skills.

WE THREE SALUTE TWO DISTINGUISHED newspaper publishers whose era extended from the 1870s into the 1950s in Northwest Arkansas. The two women blazed trails in public affairs.

Maud Dunlap Duncan, Winslow
(1873-1958)
Roberta Waugh Fulbright, Fayetteville
(1874-1953)

Maud's *Winslow American* championed the 19th Amendment that gave women the right to vote. Elected mayor of the mountain town in 1925, Maud and her "petticoat government" drew national attention and readers subscribed to her weekly newspaper from distant places.

Roberta Fulbright paid homage to Maud describing her as "a tiny piece of inspired humanity who embodies the spirit of the hills, the quality of its rocks." In July 1953 the Washington County Historical Society, named Maud "distinguished citizen" in recognition of her achievements and exceptional qualities.

IN HER OWN RIGHT, Roberta spoke out against corruption in local politics in the 1930s, and later she initiated an organization for Arkansas press women. A *Washington Post* editorial writer labeled Roberta "an imposing woman of strong features, strong views and a strong will." Not unlike her famous son Senator J. William Fulbright, Roberta had much to say about a wide range of topics. Her "As I See It" column appeared on the editorial page of the daily *Northwest Arkansas Times* for nearly 20 years, *1933 to 1952.*

IN 1897, Winslow was a sleepy little village atop the Ozarks' Boston Mountains. Seeking escape from the heat of the river valley that July, Dr. Albert Dunlap with his ailing wife and their orphaned niece, 13-year old Maud, moved from Fort Smith to the mountains and heralded Winslow's transformation into a flourishing summer resort. They had arrived as paying passengers in the caboose of a Frisco freight train.

Here Maud grew to adulthood and led an active if not trouble-free life. She soon began teaching school, obtained a pharmacist license in 1906, operated a drug store for her uncle, Dr. Dunlap, but sold it after his death in 1910. Her first husband abandoned his family in 1897; their two daughters died as children.

Maud had her first marriage annulled in 1901, and seven years later married an energetic newspaperman. It was a happier marriage cut short by death.

When Gilbert Duncan died of pneumonia in 1918, Maud assumed responsibility for the weekly *Winslow American,* and persevered with it for more than thirty years.

Through the years Maud handset her paper from type cases, printed it on a foot pedal-powered press, folded some 400 copies by hand, and delivered local copies to subscribers. The rest she mailed to a readership that extended to nearly every state. Born on her grandfather's Washington County farm, she died at 84 in a Fayetteville nursing home and was buried in Winslow clutching in her hand the final issue of *The Winslow American.*

IN 1946, ROBERTA — mother of the Senator and five other Fulbrights — was named Arkansas Mother of the Year. She had taught school and attended the University of Missouri, Columbia, for two years. Her husband Jay died in 1923 when she was 49. Roberta assumed responsibility for Fulbright enterprises that included a newspaper, banks, a hotel and other properties. Like Maud, she lost a daughter in 1925. By 1945, she had relinquished most business responsibilities to her son-in-law (Hal Douglas), but continued as publisher of the newspaper.

Roberta made *The Northwest Arkansas Times* a profitable venture; by 1949 countywide circulation had reached 9,000 and her annual payroll $100,000. Although Roberta was not a child of privilege, like the Washington Post's Katharine Graham, she achieved great respect as a publisher and columnist.

The first of five children born to a Missouri farm couple, Roberta died in 1953 of a heart ailment. She was 78. The Senator said of his mother: "Her one big love besides her family was that newspaper." Pertinent quotes by and about Roberta are sprinkled like spice throughout this book.

WHEN I CONCEIVED the idea for a Book of Columns by my favorite columnist friends in Northwest Arkansas, I did not intend to be among the featured writers. Two other column writers were interested but defaulted, one after the other. I decided to go forward with material at hand and am proud to represent the connecting generation between these four talented women writers— Maud and Roberta and Anita and Cynthia.

Welcome and happy journey through *VOICES* — our tribute to newspaper columnists past, present and future.

Jean Strong, Editor
Bentonville, Arkansas
May 2002

"A Free Press and a democratic government are an original pair, not comparable to the Garden of Eden and original sin, maybe, but just about."
--ROBERTA FULBRIGHT, 8 OCTOBER 1946

1. HEADLINE EVENTS

John Wayne, a Lost Icon?

Cynthia Haseloff, Morning News, August 2000

TALKING to a group of young adult readers at the Springdale library recently, I thought I was relating to them quite nicely when a hand went up.

"Yes," said I confidently.

"Who is John Wayne?" asked the bright-faced youngster.

Well, the impossible had happened—another icon lost to Pokemon and pals. As a teacher, I was prohibited theoretically from teaching the Bible, but not from teaching Pokemon or Star Wars. Every elementary school shows hours of animated features each year, but there was great fear that someone might be offended, some religious boundary overstepped with the mere mention of the Bible.

No one seemed to think about the necessity for openness in learning, the requisite eagerness in the learner's mind to know diverse things, to catch up with the world around and before him. No one noted how significant that that literary and spiritual classic had been to Western Civilization.

Not as a Bible-thumper, but as a teacher, a writer, and a reader I recognize that without knowledge of the Bible, you really can't read and understand much of our literature or the culture in which we swim.

For instance, someone mentions a David-Goliath conflict in business or politics. Who is David? Who is Goliath? They are part of our culture over thousands of years—not fleeting successes manufactured to reap commercial profit.

John Wayne was just a movie star, right? So what's all the fuss? Wayne was indeed a film star. But he became one over time. He did not arrive full-blown after careful marketing research and image development. He made good movies year after year. He showed up, came to stand for something. He represented an idea of America—honorable and right because of his characters' and his own commitment. He embodied the best of the western genre of literature. John Wayne didn't

Chapter 1a

John Wayne is the subject and title of a long and interesting biography published in 1995. Authors Randy Roberts and James S. Olson explained: "Middle America grew up with him in the late 1920s and 1930s, went to war with him in the 1940s, matured with him in the 1950s, and kept the faith with him in the 1960s and 1970s.

"He was *so* American, *so* like his country—big, bold, confident, powerful, loud, violent, and occasionally overbearing, but simultaneously forgiving, gentle, innocent, and naïve, almost childlike. In his person and in the persona he so carefully constructed, middle America saw itself, its past, and its future. John Wayne was his country's alter ego." (The Free Press)

Marion 'Duke' Morrison was born in Winterset (Madison County) Iowa in 1907. Hollywood changed his name in 1929 for a starring movie role. He died in 1979 in Los Angeles from lung cancer. John Wayne made 250 films during his long career and received Best Actor Oscar in 1969 for his performance as Rooster Cogburn in *True Grit*, "an Arkansas story by Charles Portis based on Judge Parker's court at Fort Smith," Cynthia reminds us.

John Wayne was closely associated with director John Ford who directed five of Cynthia's favorite Wayne movies:
Fort Apache, 1948
She Wore a Yellow Ribbon, 1949
Rio Grande, 1950
The Quiet Man, 1952
The Searchers, 1956
~~

take a poll to see where he stood. He knew. He had a cultural heritage that did not stem from corporations or from political correctness or analysis paralysis.

As a society, we have already invented the wheel. It's a done deal called civilization. But some self-righteous, sanctimonious and greedy folk are trying to do it again. Experimenting with square wheels and octagonal ones results in a bumpy ride. You can't throw out the past without endangering the future.

Yes, religion has made mistakes. People burned at the stake. People of different faiths were excluded or killed. Still happens. Science has made mistakes. Bombs were built, people used in experiments. Genetic research, unmitigated by values, can lead to violations we can not yet imagine.

Government has made a multitude of mistakes too— compromises with slavery, segregation, discrimination, fraud and lies. Few of us believe our government is a frugal, fair or faultless benefactor. But it is ours, the best there is. We understand we must keep our eye on them all. We know that because of our cultural heritage.

So this week instead of getting the kids a Pokemon movie, sit down together. Watch a John Wayne film. Read a western story together. There are some great ones about the growth of this country.

Support cultural continuity. Ask your librarian to recommend some books and movies. As Earnest Haycox said, "Westerns are an honorable entertainment." ★

~ Comments ~

Chapter 1a continued

Numerous Internet web sites offer information about "John Wayne," including "current month TV schedules" for his movies.

Arkansas claims **Broncho Billy Anderson** (1880-1971) as its cowboy star of silent movies. In April 2002 Gilbert M. "Broncho Billy" Anderson was among those inducted into The Hall of Great Western Performers in Oklahoma City. In 1903 he played several parts in the notable 12-minute film, *The Great Train Robbery,* and went on to direct and star in more than 300 films.

John Wayne may have been best but "Broncho Billy" was the first American cowboy in Hollywood, according to a 2001 tourism promotion on Arkansas public television.

~~

"The race is not always to the swift . . . but to those who keep on running."
—Cynthia's e-mail

All Politics Is Yokel

Arkansas Press Association Award Winner
Anita French, Benton County Daily Record, April 1999

CAN you imagine what must be going through the minds of those who are considering running for president of the United States? Surely, they are frantically rifling through all their records, making sure they have done none of the following:

1. Failed to pay nanny taxes. Made shady investments. Made questionable investments. Made any investments. Made a killing in the stock market. Only the pure and rich are supposed to do this, preferably male, and certainly not some uppity woman.

2. Caused "pain" in their marriage. We want only those people who have had pain-free connubialism. Or is that cannibalism? Same difference.

3. Had anything to do with anything that has the word "water" in it.

4. It would also help if they made perfect grades in school, were an orphan (or even better, born in a pod), have a spouse with no mind of her, or his, own, and have no one working for them who does stupid stuff, and they don't do stupid stuff, either.

Well, that lets me out just in the last category alone. I shudder to think what the media would make of my finances, if I had any.

"Ms. French, your latest bank statement shows you had a balance of 88 cents. Where has your money gone?"

"With the wind, Bub, with the wind."

"We notice on your tax return that you list no savings interest. Are you trying to tell us you have no savings?"

"What's a 'saving'?"

"Are you saying you have no money set aside?"

"Does a jar of pennies count?"

"Candidate woman suddenly remembers stashing away copper," the headline would read. It's reached a point where political parties will have to set up screening committees to

~ Comments ~

"No one really loves to pay taxes. Yet we know (taxes) are the lifeblood of government everywhere. Time was when there were no public roads, no public schools, and no post offices."
—Roberta Fulbright, 1938

Chapter 1b

Q. What were you thinking when you wrote about politics?
Anita: "I hate to confess this, but I love politics, although I can't necessarily say the same about politicians. I find it endlessly fascinating, outrageous, frustrating, maddening, and often hilarious. I wrote this during President Clinton's first term when the **Whitewater** controversy was raging. But we won't talk about the media and how it handles politics. Yecch!

"As I say elsewhere in this book, I came from a dysfunctional family that can't even agree on politics. My father is a Yellow-Dog Democrat, my younger brother is a Libertarian, my husband is a Republican, I am an Independent, my daughter is a Liberal, and my son votes like his mother tells him to. (He's such a good boy.)"
~~
Editor's Note: 'Yellow-Dog Democrat' today is a compliment to one who remains a true Democrat, no matter what. The term dates back to the 1928 election when southern Democrats voted for their party's presidential choice, Al Smith, although they didn't like him. [I had to look it up.]
~~

weed out candidates who have a past. They need to find people who were born yesterday, preferably as an adult. That may prove to be a problem since this hasn't been done since the Garden of Eden.

Speaking of that, has it occurred to you that most if not all of our biblical patriarchs wouldn't be presidential material themselves? I can hear the media's questions now.

"Mr. Abraham, isn't it true that during a sojourn in Egypt you lied to the pharaoh about your wife being your sister? And, is your wife your sister?"

"Mr. Moses, a search of the records reveals that you once lived in a palace but chose to leave to go live among a poor and afflicted people. Doesn't this indicate some emotional instability on your part? And did you have anything to do with those plagues that came on Egypt?

"Mr. King David" . . . Come to think of it, David wouldn't be in the running. This warrior-poet, called "a man after God's own heart," once committed adultery and then arranged for the death of his paramour's husband.

No political party would touch him. «

~ Comments ~

Chapter 1b continued

Jean: "Anita and I recently read the book, *Washington*, by **Meg Greenfield** and recommend it for its insights into the lives and work of politicians and journalists in our nation's capital. Being elected a representative or senator, says Meg, 'is not the prescription for a grounded, serene life let alone an ethically irreproachable one.'

"The late Ms. Greenfield was a *Newsweek* columnist and respected long-time editor of the Washington Post's editorial and op-ed pages. She died before her book was finished but had asked her friends to see it into print. (Public Affairs, New York, 2001)

"In the Foreword **Katharine Graham**, her friend and boss, described Meg as 'smart, wise, perceptive about people' with 'rock solid moral and ethical standards.' Historian **Michael Beschloss** wrote in the Afterword that a central theme of the book is 'how to live at the center of political and journalistic influence in Washington without losing your principles, detachment, or individual human qualities . . . Meg managed the rare feat of being a public person for thirty years without turning into one of the Washington creatures she depicts in this book."

> *"People vote Democratic so they can live like Republicans."*
> —Anita Creech quoting Bill Clinton who was quoting Harry Truman.

Launching a Rodeo Wasn't Easy

Cynthia Haseloff, Morning News, June 2000

ORIGINATING a rodeo meant hard work and some disappointments. The first rodeo attempted in Springdale during September of 1926 was dubbed "a most unusual form of entertainment" by the local newspaper and an unfortunate cold snap kept the crowds away.

The second attempt in 1945—nearly 20 years later—launched the Rodeo of the Ozarks we know today. My dad, Tommie Haseloff, and his horse Lindy made the trip from our home in Cave Springs to participate in one of the early rodeos before we moved to Springdale.

As a businessman himself and a Chamber of Commerce member and president, my father believed fiercely in the city-building potential of the annual event. Rodeo and parades, with him and his sound system, became the focus of our family Fourths.

But the 1945 rodeo—described by retired journalist Jean Strong in the Rodeo Hall of Fame publication (*The Ketchpen*, Spring 1999)—differed somewhat from later rodeos that I remember.

Two construction workers from Oklahoma suggested a local rodeo to the manager of the Welch Grape Juice plant where the men were assisting with a remodeling. Walter Watkins referred them to the two men who owned the sale barn saying those men could put it over if they went for the idea. Dempsey Letsch and Shorty Parsons went for the idea in a way that changed this Arkansas town.

With the help of the Clarence Beely American Legion Post and many other citizens, Letsch and Parsons began transforming the empty lot next to their sale barn into a rodeo arena. T.W. "Bill" Kelly from Oklahoma rounded up the livestock and 20 performers. Small portable bleachers were rented from the University of Arkansas. A long heavy rain postponed activities on opening day.

Finally a capacity crowd gathered on Wednesday afternoon for bull riding, the most exciting event. A scared Brahma bull with Sampson Sullivan aboard charged into the muddy arena. It bucked. It twisted. It threw Sullivan, then stepped squarely on his chest.

~ Comments ~

> "A town should build upon the rock of honesty [and] fair dealing, not eternal bickering and jealousies."
> —Roberta Fulbright, 1941

Chapter 1c

Twelve thousand manufacturing jobs have driven growth in **Springdale** whose population increased by 15,857 over ten years. The 2000 census counted 45,798 persons.

~~

Cynthia: "The annual Rodeo of the Ozarks in **Springdale**, Arkansas is the result of 56 years of dedicated community involvement. When the books closed for contestant registration in the year 2000, 48 saddle bronc riders, 48 bare back bronc riders, 64 bull riders, 68 calf ropers, 60 steer wrestlers, and 72 barrel racers had signed up to compete." The 2002 rodeo will be the fifty-eighth.

~~

Q. Cynthia, how does one pronounce your last name?
"Many say Hassle-hoff because of the actor, but my name is Hah-suh-loff — three syllables like ocelot and no 'h'." ['loff,' not 'hoff.']

~~

> *Effort: Some people dream of worthy accomplishments while others stay awake and do them.*
> —Cynthia's e-mail

Horrified, the crowd rose as one. The shifting weight of three hundred people caused the bleachers to collapse without warning onto the soggy ground. When the mayhem was unscrambled, seven fans shared Sullivan's 12-mile ambulance ride to the hospital. In spite of his injuries, the cowboy insisted on getting back in time for the evening performance. After all, he was competing for a $25 War Bond.

Undaunted by inclement weather and dangerously inadequate seating, the townspeople moved ahead with a bigger plan for the 1946 event. Cofounder Shorty Parsons assumed the debt for installing 5,500 permanent bleacher seats and lights for nighttime performances. American Legion members constructed box seats along the sides of the arena.

Like medicine shows of the Old West, booster caravans sold their product in outlying towns. Ticket sales reached sixteen thousand dollars, and 30,000 rodeo fans attended the four-day celebration in 1946.

The successful event prompted a group of citizens to form a non-profit organization — The Springdale Benevolent Amusement Association (SBAA) — to run the rodeo and provide benefits to the community.

The SBAA purchased the rodeo grounds from Parsons and Letsch. Town leaders Harvey Jones and John Tyson served consecutively as president for the first two years.

In 1954 then-president Parsons announced that the SBAA was "completely out of debt," a significant accomplishment in only nine years and an example for rodeo boards to come.

As Springdale tripled in size, the rodeo also grew steadily. Chamber of Commerce directors like Don Hoyt and Lee Zachary and other civic leaders worked to draw bigger crowds and national recognition.

Large corporate sponsors contributed prize money; higher payouts attracted top performers. The Professional Rodeo Cowboy Association and the Women's Professional Rodeo Association began to honor winnings and points earned at the Springdale event in determining their world champions.

The board of directors has consistently worked to keep the rodeo in the black and to improve both the physical stadium and the performances.

Since its tumultuous start in 1945 the event continues as one of Springdale's traditions every July 1 to 4. ★

They Weren't Expendable

Anita French, Daily Record, April 1995

ON the front lawn of a local National Guard armory sits a World War II tank that has seen better days. The tank faces outward, its cannon aimed at some unseen enemy.

The dull green armored plate isn't that much worse for wear but a glimpse into the tank's interior is another story. Rust has broken out inside this monolith. Like an untreated rash, it creeps up metal tubes, spreads out over the pedals and wheels, and has almost completely claimed everything once painted sterile white.

The only things that have escaped the rust are the few brass items inside the tank. They are burnished a deep gold now but are immune to erosion.

The same could be said for the memories of World War II veterans. One was with me when we stopped to look at the tank this day and he commented wryly, "Hot in the summer and cold in the winter. They weren't built for beauty or comfort."

No, they were built to kill the enemy outside and protect those inside. It's one thing to see these hulking war machines in the movies or pictures; it's another thing to see one up close. The noise they must have made when spewing artillery is unimaginable.

"It's not like anything you've heard before," my friend said. He couldn't describe it, anymore than he could make me understand what it was like to serve in a war. He could point at the different knobs, dials and levers inside the tank and tell me what they were for. He could show me where the hatch was and how the driver sat at one side and the gunner on the other.

But he couldn't tell me what it was like to be trapped in one of those things while artillery went off all around you. He can't tell me what it felt like to march all day and night in the rain, or get so tired that you learn to sleep anywhere, anytime and in any position. He can't make us understand the feeling he and his buddies had for each other—how they thought about each other's life before their own.

He can only try to describe what it was like to serve on an island where the beach was made of white coral, the water

~ Comments ~

Chapter 1d

Q: Anita, tell us about the veteran with whom you viewed the WWII tank?
"My second and current husband was the veteran who was with me this day. We weren't married and had known each other for only a few months.

"I think I learned more about veterans and the hardships they endured during this one incident than any other time. Since our marriage, I have learned even more. Frankly, I don't know how they survived, except by the grace of God."

~~

"Do you believe in love at first sight ... or should I walk by you again?"
—Anita's e-mail

~~

was a deep blue, and how a lonely 18-year-old soldier stood watch during the night, wishing someone was with him to share the sight of a silver moon shining on that white coral, that blue water.

These memories and thousands like them are shared and understood only by veterans. In a way they belong to a closed society—not willingly but because no one can understand unless they were there.

There's a scene from the classic film "The Best Years of Our Lives," about returning WWII veterans. One of them, a former bombardier, finds hundreds of abandoned fighter planes lined up, ready for the scrap heap. He climbs aboard and his combat days come rushing back. All around him, however, he sees a world that is trying to forget the war and those who served in it.

The day is coming when our WWII veterans will be gone, and their memories with them. As we observe the 50th anniversary of the end of that war, here's hoping we never forget those who gave us the best years of their lives. ★

2. The Neighborhood

The Sound of Silence Is Golden

Anita French, Daily Record, May 1995

THE streets are alive with the sound of music. Have you heard it, that loud "ba-boom, ba-boom, ba-boom" that comes rumbling out of cars? It seems some drivers want to share their musical epiphany with us. They come cruising down the street with the car windows rolled down and the radio or tape player turned up so loud it makes your ears bleed.

And what a noise it is, I should tell you. It gives new meaning to the word "mega-hurts." I don't even want to hear Pavarotti at that pitch, let alone that hellish clanking of metal the Twinkie generation has been raised on.

Isn't there some environmental law they're breaking? For punishment, they should be sealed up in their cars and made to listen to Buck Owens caterwaul at a thousand decibels.

No doubt these are the same motorists who squeal their car tires when taking off from a dead stop, and slam on their brakes when coming to one. "I am brainless. Hear me roar."

Whatever happened to goodwill toward men and peace on earth? Why can't we have a little peace and quiet around here? Why do people think they must have the radio, television or something blaring? Why do they have to share?

This fear of silence has even infected the telephone. Somewhere in the upper rooms of mindless management, it was decided that when telephone callers are put on hold, they must hear music. Any music. And since they don't know the caller's musical taste, they try to be both hip and square by letting you listen to Mantovani playing "I Can't Get No Satisfaction."

Whenever this happens, assume one of two things. You are going to be left on hold until the receiver grafts to your ear, or the company is afraid if you are left in quiet for more than a minute, you'll go insane.

We carry around noise like a security blanket. It validates our existence. "I hear that racket, therefore I am." We've gone beyond the old philosophical question: Does a tree make a sound when it falls in the forest if no one is there to hear it?

~ Comments ~

Chapter 2a

Anita: "Whatever happened to goodwill toward men and peace on earth? Why can't we have a little peace and quiet around here? Why do people think they must have the radio, television or something blaring? Why do they have to share?"
~~

Senior citizens often are criticized for deficiencies of the modern world. We take responsibility for all we have done, and do not blame others.

When you think about it, you realize it was NOT seniors who took the:
Melody out of music,
Pride out of appearance,
Romance out of love,
Commitment out of marriage,
Responsibility out of parenthood.

Togetherness out of the family,
Learning out of education,
Service out of patriotism,
Religion out of school.

Civility out of behavior.
Refinement out of language,
Dedication out of employment, or
Prudence out of spending.
~~

Now it's, if the tree does make a sound and I don't hear it, does that mean I'll get lost in the forest?

Heaven forbid we should not hear every tree that falls. It's gotten so bad that if you walked into a room and turned off the noise, everyone would jump at the sound of silence. We've become addicted to noise. If you banned it, people would sneak outside and ease their withdrawal by pressing a ghetto blaster against their ear.

We don't need any new laws. What we need is Miss Dobson. She was the town librarian where I grew up. Make any noise around her and she put on a forbidding frown, placed a rigid finger to her lips, and hissed, "Sssssh!"

What we need is an Earth's librarian. ★

~ Comments ~

Chapter 2a continued

Editor's Note: Growth unbridled can lead to chaos. The trends in recent years have prompted leaders to look beyond their own backyards and develop regional plans.

The Northwest Arkansas Regional Airport (XNA) at Highfill became a reality in the 1990s. In the 21st century wastewater treatment and pollution are problems to be solved on a regional basis.

~~

Good Fences Make Good Neighbors

Cynthia Haseloff, Morning News, July 2000

ROBERT Frost's mender of New England rock wall fences observed, "Good fences make good neighbors." Last week I looked seriously at fences along a country road I often drive. I hadn't thought much about them beyond noticing which fences were neat and in good repair and which wobbled over the hills like drunks, with posts aslant and wires sagging around their knees.

All of us notice the pretty places and the eyesores. That's all I had really thought about fences. But suddenly there were miles of fences, a lot of different kinds of fences: pipe and wood and wire and vinyl.

Each one says something quite clearly to our eyes as we speed by. They tell us important things about the people who live beyond these fences without gates, gates without fences, and fences with all sides and gates.

The fences without gates make a statement about taste. They decorate the land, can have no other purpose since nothing is kept in or out. One suspects the owner is friendly, laid back, not too eager to get out and open and close the gate with each coming and going. These fences open their arms to let you enter.

A variation on this type of fence personality is the low fence, cut off to let you see the house. This fence suggests pride of ownership and thoughtfulness on the part of the owner. It is irritating to drive by a house or field of horses with a fence board exactly at eye level.

Fences without gates, low fences without gates, and the single sided fence, usually across the front, seem to me to reveal people living in two worlds. They live in a modern busy world with no time for gates and no livestock, yet hold a place in their hearts for a traditional world in which a fence speaks of the property holder's possession and care.

The frugal farmer in me wonders about the expense of building and maintaining a fence that is without utilitarian purpose. They may be worthy in other ways I do not know.

~ Comments ~

> *"Fences tell us important things about the people who live beyond."*
> — Cynthia Haseloff

Chapter 2b

Planners estimated that by 2001 total **population** in our two counties had approached **329,000**—an increase from the 311,121 people counted in the 2000 census. That computes to an increase of about 1,000 people per month.

~~

Benton County had two thousand more women than men but men outnumbered women by 307 in Washington County. (2000 census)

~~

There are also gates without fences, standing across a drive like arms crossed over the chest. They say clearly 'Stay out.' Be warned. Drive on. This is not someone to mess with.

Never drive around this fenceless gate—a humorless, probably abused (by vandals and poachers), already angry, possibly armed person waits beyond. Call ahead.

Fences with gates. The owners of these seem to be particularly well balanced and organized, grounded in reality, clear thinkers all around. They know the purpose of a fence and a gate.

A fence and gate keep things out and in. These are complex people often having fences within fences—all with good gates or cattle guards. They may even have a gateless fence to allow access to the inner system of working fences.

I admire a good fence with wires tight or rails secure. I love a gate, on hinges that swing free, and goes exactly where it should. A bad gate is one thing I am not romantic about.

I don't want a relationship with a gate. I want it to work. ★

~ Comments ~

"If you are a writer, you locate yourself behind a wall of silence and no matter what you are doing, driving a car or walking or doing housework, which I love, you can still be writing, because you have that space."
— Joyce Carol Oates (quoted in Jade Walker's web site Ezine, *The Written Word*)

Chapter 2b continued

Novelist Cynthia Haseloff finds such space while she works with her animals as well as when doing housework or training her Appaloosa pony named Pabot'an ('Little Horse' in Kiowa). On really trying days she goes to a movie to regain her equilibrium.

"The author . . . writes all day long, when he is thinking, when he is reading, when he is experiencing."
— Somerset Maugham

Love and Marriage

Jean Strong, The Independent, December 1949

A romantic glow hung over the entire nation when Vice President Alben Barkley made the trip to the altar with Jane Hadley two weeks ago. That glow lingered over Center Point last week, as three of your friends and mine were married. The events made November seem more like June despite the rain, snow and ice that alternately covered the ground. Two of the weddings took place on Thanksgiving Day when Rosemary Trickey married Bill Mullaney at Iowa Falls, and Ramona Gordon married Gene Sells at Cedar Rapids. Rosemary taught in the high school here last year and Ramona is the current kindergarten teacher.

I drove to Iowa Falls with two friends for Rosemary's wedding. We left Center Point at 7:20 but were late for the 10 A.M. wedding. The roads were covered with ice and snow and rain fell intermittently.

By 9 o'clock, creeping along at 30 miles per hour, we were 60 miles from our destination. Luckily the last 25 miles of paving weren't icy. We made good time and were only 15 minutes late. We missed part of the ceremony but enjoyed all of the "immediately following" to which the invitations had requested the honor of our presence.

After the 200 guests had wished Rosemary and Bill "the best of luck and happiness" and Rosemary had kissed nearly everyone in return, we all sat down to a delicious turkey dinner. For the benefit of Rosemary's many friends who didn't attend the wedding, I can say that she was as vivacious and charming as ever and looked extremely happy with her new husband.

The third wedding took place Saturday night right here in Center Point when Betty Newman and John Henderson said their sacred vows. John gets credit for the best bridegroom performance. He didn't get out of step once, nor muff his lines. I heard from a reliable source that this was John's fifth trip to the altar; the first four times were as best man. That explains why he nearly missed his cue to kiss the bride! ★

~ Comments ~

> *"Marriage, we'll say, is a very complicated machine with heavy wheels and light bearings."*
> —Roberta Fulbright

Chapter 2c

Jean: "Rosemary Trickey and I were students at Iowa but we met in Chicago in 1947. We both had summer jobs aboard the *SS City of Grand Rapids* that steamed daily from Chicago to Benton Harbor, Michigan. The pleasure boat berthed each night beneath the Michigan Avenue Bridge following a moonlight cruise.

"Rosemary and I were among the dozen men and women students recruited at Iowa. My memoirs will include a chapter about that summer because it contributed much to the education of this Iowa farm girl. Passengers boarding for the daytime cruise were greeted nearly every day by the ship orchestra's rendition of 'Peg o' My Heart.'

"Disparate groups like the Moody Bible Institute and the Whiskey Dealers' Convention booked daytime outings, on different days, of course. The gaming tables and slot machines were locked away when the Bible people came on board. For the Whiskey Dealers, our student bartenders had mixed popular drinks in tubs and bottled them for fast dispensing.

"Staterooms for paying passengers were available on upper decks, and tasty meals were served in the ship's dining room. Three hearty meals a day plus the midnight snack bar were appreciated benefits for student employees. Our accommodations were tiny staterooms for two with stacked bunk beds and one chest of drawers. I used the wall drop-down seat for writing letters home describing daily activities aboard ship that seemed fascinating during my first month on board."

Our NW Arkansas Neighborhood

Jean Strong, VOICES, 2002

AS an Iowa transplant in Arkansas for the past 11 years, I have watched and read about the changes taking place. A recent (2/24/02) supplement to the Sunday *Arkansas Democrat Gazette*, Northwest Edition, contained a bonanza summary about the past, present and future of the region. News reporters and editors from three papers — Democrat *Gazette*, Daily *Record* and NW Arkansas *News* — reported their findings under the title: "Winds of Change across the Ozark Plateau."

What do residents like most about our area? The short answers are 'Quality of Life' and a 'Small-town Environment.' Specifically we appreciate the beauty, great views, clean look and smell, a good place to raise children.

And I am among those who will tell you it is also a wonderful retirement haven. I found NW Arkansas during a search in 1989-90 when I was ready to leave my home in Washington, DC after nearly 18 years.

In the 1990s our two counties of Benton and Washington were "among the fastest growing regions in the nation," and the towns of Farmington and Prairie Grove joined the urban area. If the trend continues, planners say, four of nine other rural towns in Washington County may become urban over the next 30 years.

An evolution in the 20th century saw the economy shift from apple export capital to an "epicenter of retailing, protein production and trucking." Bentonville (2000 population 19,730) grew by 28.5 percent in ten years while Benton County's population increased 57 percent. In 2001 Wal-Mart, with headquarters in Bentonville, became the largest company in the world.

"The prevailing idea in Ozark culture is that if you have wealth, you don't flaunt it," according to University anthropology professor Mary Jo Schneider. Our area has more than its share of millionaires and billionaires, and the Sam Walton family has helped maintain that standard. ★

~ Comments ~

Chapter 2d

The **University of Arkansas** is the biggest developer in **Fayetteville** while **Bentonville** and **Lowell** are home to corporate giants — Wal-Mart, Tyson Foods and J. B. Hunt Trucking.

~~

Springdale boasts 12,000 manufacturing jobs and the late long-term mayor, Charles N. McKinney, played a key role in creating those jobs and public works projects like the city's Industrial Park and Shiloh Museum.

McKinney's final resting-place is in the city-owned cemetery where notable industrialists—John Tyson, Joe Steele and Harvey Jones—are also buried.

~~

Rogers, following a city plan, has annexed land west of the city toward the I-540 corridor. Developers are busy transforming that rural landscape.

It is possible that this multi-culture city will become a premiere center of retail and office commerce in coming years, surpassing Fayetteville.

~~

Other smaller communities in the area have their share of industries and businesses large and small, all contributing to the economy and all facing challenges in providing infrastructure and service.

Bentonville Mayor Terry Coberly said, "The most difficult problem we face is how to keep up with the infrastructure in a way that allows the least amount of disruption to that small-town atmosphere loved by so many."

~~

3. GETTING ACQUAINTED

Cruising in California

Anita French, Herald-Democrat, December 1993

When Miami, Florida passed a law in 1993 to ban "unnecessary, repetitive driving," the news story triggered a column for Anita French, who wrote:

MIAMI has outlawed "cruising," the aimless and ritualistic pastime of teenagers that has been around since the 1950s, and before, probably. Cruising. How that brings back memories. When I was growing up in San Fernando, California, cruising was as much a part of teenage life as teased hair, pimples, and Dippity-Do. By the time I reached high school in the late 1950s, my fellow teenagers and I must have logged more miles than daily coast-to-coast flights.

The most famous cruising street in America—Van Nuys Boulevard—was about 10 miles out of town. This was the backdrop of that paean to teenagers, director George Lucas' _American Graffiti._

While that movie was set during the 1970s, we 1950 California girls and boys were their role models.

Van Nuys Boulevard was the undisputed champion—the El Camino Real of cruising. You might cruise around in your own town, but Van Nuys Boulevard was where you headed if you were serious about it.

For teenagers Van Nuys Boulevard was serious business. Guys made sure their cars were in "cherry" condition before setting a tire on that sacred boulevard. Countless coats of wax had to be applied until the car was so shiny it dazzled. The chrome had to gleam and wink.

The inside was as clean as any teenager's mother despaired of ever seeing her child's room. And if the muffler made a nice low roar, that was even better. If you drove a low-rider, there was just a whiff of danger that drove girls wild.

Wasn't that why guys cruised? To pick up chicks? There was another reason, although they were too macho to admit it. (While not a '50s word, "macho" is as old as Adam.) The guys wanted other guys to admire and envy their cars. Having

~ Comments ~

> "Knowing that women will forever do much that has to be done, I wish sometimes that men did like women in high places because they have the ability and willingness, but there just isn't enough ego to go around and men cannot function without it."
> —Roberta Fulbright

Chapter 3a

About ANITA
During a newspaper career that flourished in her middle years, **Anita French Creech** has written columns for two weeklies and two daily newspapers in northwest Arkansas. She is now a business writer for _The Morning News_.

Anita has an associate's degree in journalism from John Brown University, **Siloam Springs**. She was in her late forties when she decided against going for a bachelor's degree "because I needed a job." She found one before graduation as a part-time reporter for a small weekly, thanks to the recommendation of her JBU counselor and teacher, Fred Lollar, a retired journalist and "wise man."

"Mr. Lollar said I didn't really need a four-year degree, as my life's experience made up for the lack of one. I attribute my career partly to him; he helped hone my writing skills and offered endless words of support and encouragement. We still keep in touch."

Anita has two children. Her older child, a son, is a talented musician when he's not working in a Siloam Springs factory. Her daughter is the museum curator at the University of Missouri in Columbia.

~~

the girls drool over them was what made the little hairs on teenage boys' chests bristle.

Teenage girls back then didn't usually drive such nice cars. If they had one at all, it was something daddy bought and it was probably a Nash Rambler. Dad was, after all, so uncool. But while we groaned about our nerdy wheels, we were more concerned with how we looked. That's why girls put on 10 different outfits before finding one that looked good enough to cruise in, and why we applied the same amount of makeup to our faces as guys did wax to their cars.

We San Fernando cruisers didn't get over to Van Nuys Boulevard often, usually saving that for the weekend. Besides, Van Nuys High School was our biggest rival in football, so we didn't like to tread on enemy territory too much.

Instead, we would cruise around town for a while, and then end up where every teenager within shouting distance ended up—Bob's Big Boy drive-in, home of the famous hamburger and the best greasy french fries and onion rings in the world.

If any parent was missing a San Fernando Valley teenager, the first place he or she looked was Bob's Big Boy. There we were, sitting in our cars, drinking chocolate Cokes, and car hopping. And I don't mean waiting on customers.

We went to Bob's to visit each other in cars. Teenage girls often came in one car and then left in another, usually with a boy driving. Some kids would drive slowly through Bob's to see who was there.

Friendships and feuds were formed at Bob's. So were engagements. It was like some weird mating game where the cars circled each other, acting like antennas for their drivers.

"Unnecessary, repetitive driving." Cities may ban it, but they'll never exorcise the ghosts of all those teenagers who spent a big part of their lives cruising down the boulevard.

It was so cool. ★

~Comments~

Chapter 3a continued

Q. How did you get started?
Anita: "I don't recall how my first column, which I wrote for *The News Leader* (later *The Herald-Democrat*) in Siloam Springs came about. I believe the editor asked me in the late 1980s if I wanted to write one. Once begun, it was assumed that I would continue at the next paper.

"When I changed employers, however, I started out by asking if I could contribute to a weekly column written at that time by different reporters.

"When that column was dropped, I asked the editor if I could write a column called GRAY MATTERS that talked about issues and things that affect seniors. Not surprisingly, I soon grew bored with that and my column evolved into a human interest one. I found that many of us share common gripes or feelings, regardless of our ages."

~~

Mothers Aren't Created Equal

Anita Creech, The Morning News, May 2000

MY FIRST husband's lasting childhood memory was watching his mother being beaten by his father while he and his older sister cowered behind a couch. His last memory of her was when she died in a hospital of kidney failure years later.

In between were the "good" years—when he and his sister lived with relatives while their mother worked as a practical nurse to support them. She was able to see her children only occasionally. Later, her grown son would silently weep when he remembered how his underpaid and overworked mother sometimes sent her little boy a card with a nickel taped inside.

My mother stayed home and chose to do so. My dad made a good living as a union man, and mom saved their money well. She prepared home-cooked meals, baked wonderful pies and sewed clothes for her children. She spent one winter making a whole new wardrobe for my doll as a Christmas present. Later, she took care of her grandchildren. Now in her 80s, she still thinks we all need looking after.

Her own mother was part Cherokee and the second wife of a Scottish preacher and Oklahoma farmer. They eked out a living raising cotton. I remember grandma as one who never interfered in her children's lives. When she became elderly, her children took turns having her stay with them. She died an invalid in her oldest daughter's home.

My other grandmother married at 14 and had her first child while still a child herself and living in Arkansas. The babies came one after another. She liked her boys the best and became fiercely partisan to them—less so for her daughters and daughters-in-law. My mother once speculated that maybe her mother-in-law's hard life made her so fearful, so censorious so . . . difficult to love. Ironically, it was a granddaughter, my cousin, who took granny in when no one else in the family could or would.

My first husband was an alcoholic. Our children grew up in an unstable, emotional household where maternal love too often took a back seat to selfishness. Somehow they managed to emerge intact but not unscathed.

~ Comments ~

Anita French Creech (1991)

Chapter 3b

Q. Do you enjoy writing a column?
Anita: "A column is a wonderful break from writing about city and school board meetings, and the other mundane issues that occupy a newspaper reporter. I don't have to give readers 'just the facts, ma'am.' In a column I can give them outrageous opinion or sarcasm or just plain nonsense, if I feel like it. Of course, I'm still subject to the same libel laws, which rein me in a little.

"And because they're my letters to readers, I resent anyone editing them except for grammar or misspelling. So what if I sound stupid? It's my byline, not the editor's."

Cynthia agrees, and Jean says, "If you are the editor and write a column you don't have that problem."
~~
Q. Who are your favorite columnists and why?
Anita: **Mike Royko** and Molly Ivins. Royko is no longer with us, of course, but I tried never to miss his column. He was so 'in your face' over what he saw

I have a friend who has always had a strained relationship with her own mother, she said. When they get together, there's little to share except small talk about family. Like many daughters, she realizes they should be closer but they will likely never cross the gulf that lies between them. Still, it's her mother.

THIS Sunday is when children are supposed to honor their mothers with cards, flowers, gifts or dinner out. I have yet to find a card that describes the complicated relationship between mothers and their children. I expect there's someone out there that feels the same way about fathers.

There are different ways—all of them accurate—to describe the women profiled here. Flawed. Loving. Self-sacrificing. Imperial—even cruel—at times. Proud. Overwhelmed. Under-appreciated. Ignorant. Blessed.

Neglectful? Maybe. Regretful? Most assuredly. They are mothers. It goes with the territory. ★

~ Comments ~

Chapter 3b continued

as the idiocy of government and/or officials. He wrote with great humor, a sense of self-mockery and compassion. I miss him, which is something all writers hope their readers would say.

"I also love to read **Molly Ivins** (most of the time) because she has a way of brushing aside all the nonsense and zeroing in on the real crux of an issue. And, like Royko, she does it with great humor.

"Finally, **Erma Bombeck**, another voice no longer heard. Has anyone ever written as humorously about the everyday problems and frustrations of families as Erma? She is irreplaceable."

~~

Editor's Note: Mike Royko (1932-1997), called 'the best' newspaper writer of his time, wrote for Chicago papers and his columns were syndicated in more than 600 U.S. newspapers. The University of Chicago Press in 1999 published selected columns from four decades in a book titled *One More Time, The Best of Mike Royko.*

~~

"*When god gave us children He gave us a job big enough and important enough to stagger the best of us. The other side of this picture is that it is the dearest task you will ever be called upon to perform.*"
—Roberta Fulbright,
17 February 1939

Confessions of a Baby Boomer

Cynthia Haseloff, Morning News, July 2000

MORE than 20 years ago I wrote a western novel with a woman as the main character. It was titled *Ride South!* My reasons for choosing to write westerns were family background, interest in the history of the American West, love of the great western films of John Ford, romanticism and idealism. But most of all I became hooked on the genre because of the values and the hope they held. I love hope.

When I began to write, the West was the perfect locale for my non-political, strong women. The West really was a place that welcomed women on their own terms. During the seventies little seemed to be on solid ground because of the major upheaval in our country's thought. Like many in the boomer generation, I took it hard.

And like many other quiet Americans, I looked for a positive something to believe in. The media and activists found little of worth about America. The western did and still does. So I joined up.

I missed many important happenings during those 20 years. One thing was the women's rights movement. When it began, it seemed silly to me. I didn't like the rhetoric that seemed hysterical; the clamor seemed to be about the right to equal stupidity rather than for the opportunity to become the best human being you could become. At home and at the girls' school I attended I was always encouraged to be whatever I could be. Women in my own family did not seem oppressed.

My grandmother who bore ten children and raised all but one could have been considered a victim of her gender. If she ever were a victim, she must have surmounted it with a deep grace. To me she was an interesting human being with an uncommon share of love, wisdom and good sense.

The women I knew did what they wanted, tempered always by that humanizing necessity of doing what needed to be done. We had family businesses in which the women were involved and essential to success. Taking care of houses, husbands and children did not seem horrible. I understood that it was not universally so, but I figured that eventually someone has to pick up the dirty clothes to wash and cook something to eat. Civilization rests on mundane things like socks in the drawer and a meal that takes as long to prepare

~Comments ~

Cynthia Haseloff (1998)

Chapter 3c

Q. Is it difficult to think of column ideas?
Cynthia: "Having a supply of topics is important to me because there will be days when inspiration does not come. It is also good to have a backlog of columns written to submit when nothing works."

~~

About CYNTHIA
Cynthia Haseloff won a Western Writers of America 'Spur Award for Best Western Novel' in 1998. She began writing an equine column titled EQUINOTES for *The Morning News* in the year 2000 while finishing her tenth novel, ***Changing Trains***.

A reviewer said of her recent work of fiction, *Changing Trains*, "Cynthia Haseloff has created another wonderful Western (novel) of character and place, beautifully plotted with characters one loves or hates, but always finds engrossing."
—Doris Meredith, *Roundup* magazine, June 2001

as to eat. This means a lot to any person or family's sense of security.

In the West of another time my heroines took on big tasks and accomplished them as human beings with skills and limitations. Many of those women never voted or held a paying job but their voices were strong in the home counsel that shaped a family.

When a man built his home two hundred miles beyond the last outpost, he respected the woman who stood beside him, his equal, fighting Indians or droughts or northers, bearing children and bringing civilization in the wagon with her Damask table cloth and the carefully protected china cups. ★

~ Comments ~

Chapter 3c continued

Formal schooling has occupied a great portion of Cynthia's life. She has three college degrees (in art and art history, and speech from the University of Arkansas, and a Ph.D in film and TV from the University of Missouri, Columbia) plus a teaching certificate. She taught high school journalism before her first novel was published in 1980.

Nine more novels and several short stories have followed. Four of the 10 are Arkansas novels: *A Killer Comes to Shiloh*, *Marauder*, *Badman* and *Dead Woman's Trail*.

Over 20 years of self-study, Cynthia has acquired a substantial knowledge of **American Indian history**.

"I used to say I lived in the twentieth century, worked in the nineteenth and planned for the twenty-first," she says. Her life work to date has centered on writing historical novels and short stories.

Cynthia is currently enrolled in her second year of law school at the University of Arkansas, Fayetteville, and expects to combine her many varied interests.

~~

Daughters of the Old West

Cynthia Haseloff, Morning News, July 2000

WHILE writing about the heroic West of the 19th century, I also missed a small group of women—never more than 700 in number—who had grown up on ranches, competed alongside men in rodeos and attracted audiences from around the U.S. These daughters of the Old West crashed into the 20th century riding broncos and bulls. They also roped and wrestled steers.

They were not Amazons—women of gigantic proportions or militant mind-sets. Some were tiny. Looking at a pair of size four boots on display at the National Cowboy and Western Heritage Museum in Oklahoma City, I wondered if their owner could actually have ridden bulls and broncos and wrestled steers. She had.

These young women were professional athletes, flesh and blood women competing in strenuous sports; yet they married and bore children. Their names were Tad Lucas and Fox Hastings, Bertha Kapernick and Reine Hafley, Marjorie and Alice Greenough, and many more.

Today's counterparts are Sherry Cervi, Charmayne James Rodham, Kay Blandford, Kristie Peterson and the woman or girl next door who spends her weekends at jackpots across the region with her eyes on a distant prize.

Hard times came to rodeo women in the 1940s. Some problems were of their own making, some stemmed from public outcry after young women died in rodeo events and some were prompted by producers like Gene Autry who thought women should dress up the rodeo—but not perform.

Ultimately excluded from competition, the cowgirls formed their own organization—the Girls Rodeo Association (GRA) that eventually in 1987 became the Women's Professional Rodeo Association (WPRA). Its members now compete in Professional Rodeo Cowboy Association events alongside the men. The WPRA is the oldest organization for professional female athletes in America. Although it is governed solely by and for women, its history remained unrecorded until 1991.

Today these women are primarily barrel racers. Like other competitors in PRCA events, they must earn their right to

~ Comments ~

Novels by Cynthia Haseloff
1980 – *Ride South!*
1981 – *Killer Comes to Shiloh*
1982 – *Marauder*
1983 – *Badman*
1984 – *Dead Woman's Trail*
1991 – *The Chains of Sarai Stone*

Kiowa Trilogy:
1992 – *Man Without Medicine*
1997 – *The Kiowa Verdict*
    (1998 Spur Award)
1998 – *Satanta's Woman*

2001 – *Changing Trains*

Chapter 3d

A reader recently queried Cynthia at her web site WWW.READWESTERNS.COM about *Marauder,* her third book. He asked about the main characters and the extent to which her stories are historical as well as fictional.

Cynthia replied: "The characters in the books, unless real historical persons, are generally fictional, but the backgrounds and many of the incidents are based upon history. The background for *Marauder* is Northwest Arkansas where the **Civil War Battle of Prairie Grove** took place. I've walked over much of the battlefield. It is well cared for. The character 'Crysop' is loosely based on John Brown. 'Rhea' is a woman of fiction based upon some early women doctors.

"Rhea may have a subconscious reincarnation as Mari Marshay in my 2001 book *Changing Trains*. This time the lady doctor is also a gambler, and the story takes place in Indian Territory. Here the history is incidental to a nice story."

compete and gaining a WPRA card does not come easily. Sometimes the women feel that they live on the interstates because, as barrel racers, they haul their own horses to every event they attend hoping to earn money and points toward an even bigger prize.

They train their own horses and temper their personal ambitions by placing the horse's care and comfort above their own needs. The horse is an athlete with fragile legs and equine instincts.

In spite of long drives and fierce competition, barrel racer Sherry Cervi—not all-around cowboy Fred Whitfield—won the most money at the 1999 National Finals Rodeo in Las Vegas. In fact she won $30,000 more than the next highest money winner.

As Baxter Black, cowboy poet, pointed out in a recent *Western Horseman* column, "Playin' by the rules, all set by men, she (Sherry Cervi) finished the season with the biggest paycheck in the PRCA. And if the (NFR) association allowed women to enter team roping, she'd probably have won enough in that event to leave Las Vegas wearin' the all-around cowboy buckle." (All-around honors go to the participant who is tops in two events.)

If you go out for popcorn after rodeo performances by point leaders Fred Whitfield or Billy Etbauer, you'll miss seeing some of the top women professionals on the circuit, and a little bit of the west's history. ★

~ Comments ~

Serenity: In the race to be better or best do not miss the joy of being.
—Cynthia's e-mail

Chapter 3d continued

Northwest Arkansas was the site of two major trans-Mississippi Battles of the Civil War. Pea Ridge is now a national military park. Prairie Grove, the focal point of *Marauder*, is a state park. **Pea Ridge** battles took place in March 1863 and the fight at **Prairie Grove** occurred 7 December that same year.

~~

Four Short Stories
by Cynthia Haseloff
Redemption at Dry Creek, 1994
Guipago's Vow, 1997
Favorite Son, 2000
Callie, 2001

New Editor in Town

Jean Strong, The Independent, September 1949

AT first glance into the office, you may think *The Independent* is a one-woman newspaper. But it's far from it and no one knows that as well as I. Volunteer and professional help are at hand.

A young high school student is interested in reporting his school's sporting events. Three local ministers bring in their church news and take a turn at writing the column titled "As We See It." Readers in nearby communities have volunteered to send news items so our coverage will extend over the surrounding towns.

Two weeks ago the "gang" at *The Marion Sentinel* pitched in to help produce our newspaper—after finishing their own paper. Their linotypist, shop foreman, pressman, and our publisher helped make-up our pages and print and fold them.

Their good help and equipment reduced the usual five-hour production job to two hours, and I was back in Center Point right after supper to address the papers for mailing. At 7 the next morning, Postmaster Street and his assistants began putting the finished product in your mailboxes. From beginning to end, your newspaper is a cooperative effort, and we hope to make it the best weekly newspaper in the state!

Weekly but hopefully yours, Editor

~ Comments ~

> *"The writing of this little column has been a great pleasure and outlet for me and you have made me happy regarding it. It has sustained me in a manner difficult to describe, yet very real to me, and difficult to get on without."*
> —Roberta Fulbright

Chapter 3e

About JEAN

Jean: "**Center Point**, Iowa originated in 1839. One hundred eleven years later it was a friendly town of some 800 people in northwestern Linn County when I was editor, manager, reporter, photographer, and janitor at the venerable weekly newspaper, *The Independent*.

"It happened for me in August 1949. Just back from a Theta Sigma Phi journalism convention in Dallas, I dropped in at the *Marion Sentinel*. Publisher Ralph Young had bought the *Sentinel* from the Papes family in 1946 and I continued to fill in as linotypist during holidays from college. Ralph had said he would buy a newspaper for me to run someday, but he surprised me with his greeting: 'Jean, I've found a newspaper (in Center Point). I'll buy it if you'll run it.' I was 16 semester hours short of graduating and wanted to finish what I'd started, but after considering his offer for a full week, I accepted, and knew I'd made the right decision after I slept well that night.

"Rather than heading back to a campus dorm, I rented a room in Center Point where I slept weeknights except Wednesdays. On Wednesday nights and on weekends I stayed at my parent's home in Cedar Rapids.

February 1950, WEEKLY BUT HOPEFULLY

ON returning from lunch Wednesday, I sat down at my big roll-top desk to lay out some ads. Suddenly, pooling water surrounded my chair. An even larger pool covered the back shop floor. Should I call the plumber or get busy with that rag-mop? R-a-g-g-m-o-p-p, that is. (I don't care for that song either!)

An SOS call brought neighbors Chippy Dufoe and Rex McAtee to the rescue, but before they arrived I waded through the gently swirling waters, detected water gushing from the wall and visualized myself benefiting from that mandatory college swimming course.

This was a job for the water superintendent and the street commissioner. Sloshing over to the phone again, I summoned Verne Carver, Center Point's treasured utility man. It didn't take the fellows long to determine the source of my waterfall and lake.

Main Street was draining into my basement office. Melting snow had found a convenient hole in the sidewalk entrance to the alley. The men quickly dug a trench to reroute the water. I am eternally grateful for their quick action and take this opportunity to thank Verne, Chippy, Rex, Wayne Wyeth and any others who assisted.

Some past issues of *The Independent* proved a good substitute for a rag-mop. We completed the day's work and got the paper out on time with nothing worse than wet feet. ★

~ Comments ~

Chapter 3e continued

"Publisher Young supplied a cash journal and a ledger for keeping accounts, and an automobile for the 18-mile weekly trip to Marion. He said I should write my weekly paycheck for forty dollars (minus taxes). I would get a percentage of the profits (if any) at the end. We soon increased circulation by 150 subscribers, from 650.

"After mailing the paper on Friday mornings, I produced letterheads and statements in my back shop for local businesses, and farmed out larger jobs to the Sentinel print shop. I also got started editing and planning for next week's *Independent*.

"Eight months later Ralph sold the *Independent* and its 800-subscriber list, at a profit, to a publisher in an adjoining county. A $700 "bonus" enabled my return to school that fall, without working a job. I continued as editor for five months with the new publisher.

~~

"I had learned back shop skills at the *Sentinel* (1943-1945) following high school graduation—linotyping, operating printing presses, and setting type out of cases as Maud Duncan was doing in **Winslow, Arkansas**. At the *Sentinel* we handset type for headlines, ads and job work that required fonts in styles and sizes not available on the Linotype machine. I remember hand-setting a letter in typewriter font that was aimed at subscribers whose subscriptions were about to expire. We had typewriters but photocopying was not available.

"The opportunity to apprentice as a Linotype operator and learn other printing skills had arisen in 1943 because men who would have filled the job had gone to war."

Reading for Fun and Profit

FOR ROSE CHRISTENSEN'S *READING COACH*
Jean Strong, Daily Record, April 1997

IN 1931 as Margaret Bourke-White with her camera was being photographed atop the Chrysler Building on a gargoyle overlooking New York City, I was in a one-room country schoolhouse learning to read. A few years later I struggled to read one of the few books available in my home, but *A Tale of Two Cities* proved beyond the ability of my years.

Not until eighth grade did I learn the pure joy of reading books. Our rural school district awarded certificates to pupils for reading a dozen books during the school year; *Black Beauty* by Anna Sewell is the one I remember.

Even in that auspicious year of 1939—when LIFE, the weekly picture magazine, was in its third year of publication—I had no clue that one day I would be reviewing, with the legend herself, the photographer's personal collection of photos.

At *Life* Bourke-White's 25-year-career as a war photographer and photojournalist was among my first story assignments (published 16 May 1955). After talking all week about her pictures and experiences, she remarked, "You know more about me than anybody." She graciously autographed my copy of her book *Passage to India* and expressed pleasure at being my first collected autograph.

At *Life*—and later at *Fortune* and Time-Life Books—I was pleased to be paid for reading. These organizations called it 'research.' Research involved reading newspapers, cables from correspondents around the world, and books—and working with photographers, writers, and layers of editors in preparing picture stories for the magazine, and chapters for books.

I discovered Samuel Eliot Morison's works, including *Admiral of the Ocean Sea*, 2 vol. (Pulitzer Prize 1943) while researching a story about Christopher Columbus (*Life*, 10 October 1955).

~ Comments ~

> No one can predict to what heights you can soar. Even you will not know until you spread your wings.
> —Cynthia's e-mail

<u>Chapter 3f</u>

Jean Strong's **40-year journalism career** took her from Cedar Rapids, Iowa to New York, Philadelphia and Washington, D.C. "I was on the staff at two magazines (*Life* and *Fortune*) and two book publishers (Farm Journal and Time-Life Books), and I'm not finished yet," she says. As a freelancer she created and published three annual promotion publications for Iowa (1964-'65-'66), a family genealogy (Strong and Oliver families) in 1978 and in 1996 the non-fiction book, *A Prairie Almanac, 1839 to 1919*. It was based on a first-person manuscript left by a pioneer ancestor. Jean is currently planning and will be writing in 2002 a 100-year illustrated history of the public library in her hometown (Marion, Iowa) for publication before 2005.

~~

Anita Creech is currently conducting interviews for a book about black families in northwest Arkansas. That book is a joint venture with Myra Moran, a bookseller who specializes in books about Arkansas.

~~

Cynthia Haseloff, of course, is working, between law classes, on at least one short story and a novel.

~~

Morison was predictably not thrilled to receive a midnight phone call from me to check the accuracy of one point the *Life* writer had added. I lost a coin toss with another researcher; the story had to be 'closed' that night and even one source— let alone the usual three to substantiate a "fact" — was not to be found. Morison himself was this researcher's last resort.

At Time-Life Books some years later, I perused extensive libraries that were assembled in-house for the various book series—World War II, the Epic of Flight, and Seafarers among them. Today I enjoy browsing shelves of local libraries and bookstores for my reading interest.

Reading, it turns out, is a portable lifetime skill one can use for enjoyment and for earning a living. In this Information Age reading rapidly and understanding what we read is ever more necessary for personal satisfaction and success. ★

~ Comments ~

Roberta Fulbright was a "Virginian by heritage, a Missourian by birth and an Arkansan by long tenure."
—Dorothy D. Stuck and Nan Snow in *Roberta—A Most Remarkable Fulbright*

4. ATTITUDE

It's My Pity Party
Anita French, Daily Record, March 1995

WHEN some people are in a funk, they go out and spend money, go home and kick the cat or eat fudge. Me, I have a pity party. There's nothing like a pity party to whine away the blues. You don't have to send out invitations because you don't need no stinkin' company. You're the hostess and the guest. Let the bad times roll.

If you've never held a pity party before, there is a certain etiquette to observe. First, you should always hold a pity party at night when things look really . . . dark. You don't want any bright, happy sunshine trying to make you feel better.

Secondly, don't dress up. Pity parties are always informal. Put on some old sweats or blue jeans, or a pair of tights that have cat hairs all over them. Wear an old shirt that has food stains on it. Go barefoot and don't brush your hair. Forget the makeup. What do you care how you look? No one loves you anyway.

Even a pity party needs entertainment though, and you can go either way here. Watch a sad movie and cry until your eyes are little puffy slits or put on some music that matches your mood.

If you're suffering from the "love blues," a good recommendation is "Never, Never Will I Marry" or "Down with Love." ("Down with love, let's liquidate all its friends...") Opera is also good, because there's almost always some neat suffering going on here—especially if it's by Verdi or Puccini. Italians know how you feel.

Wagner is dandy if you're plotting revenge. His music makes you feel like taking up a sword and slaying some Valkyries.

Heavy classical music never fails either. I find Rachmaninoff's Piano Concert No. 2 works well at plumbing the depths of your suffering.

Be sure to unplug the phone or take it off the hook during your pity party. After all, you're moanin' low here, and you certainly don't want to be interrupted by friendly chatter as if all's right with the world. It might be someone who says, "I

"One of the things mother left me—just try to be fair. It's true one never achieves it, but it's one of the things worth working for as long as one lives."
—Roberta Fulbright

Chapter 4a

Q. Why did you write this column?
Anita: "I wrote the Pity Party column several days after becoming upset over the way someone close to me had hurt my feelings. I did put on the record player, selecting songs that matched my mood and devising all sorts of vengeful scenes in my mind. And I actually did wear leggings with cat hairs all over them. After a few days, of course, I had recovered from my self-imposed snit and began to see the humor in what I had done. Thus, the column."

~~

"We cannot change the direction of the wind, but we can adjust our sails."
—Anita's e-mail

feel your pain." All that does is make you want to be sure they do, preferably with a solid left to their sloping forehead.

Don't plan on a pity party lasting too long, however. There's just something about life that ruins a pity party and, before long, the party's over, my friend.

Don't you hate it when that happens? ★

Bad Attitude Makes Losers

Cynthia Haseloff, Morning News, June 2000

LAST weekend I watched a fast pitch girls' softball tournament at Lake Fayetteville rather than a horse event. Many of the kids were stunners—disciplined athletes in shin guards and French braids with hair ribbons. They paid attention to their coaches, knew what was going on around them and ran to catch every fly or grounder even in practice.

By late Sunday afternoon, even the best were flagging. Asked how many games they had played, one of the Blazers replied, "We've played a lot." Hooray for Title Nine and the young women who have made good use of it!

However some of the kids were losers—not because they didn't win, not because they didn't have the opportunity to play, or the time, equipment and coaches, and parental and community support. It was their bad attitudes.

They were slovenly, ignoring what went on in the game and during practice. The triumph of their day was stealing golf balls off the nearby driving range. They cared about nothing except themselves. If a softball landed in their mitts, they would have dropped it to prove they didn't care.

In our grandmother's day this "I don't care" attitude would reap a quick swat and a long talk. Grandma knew what a killer attitude could be.

As adults today we spend a lot of time trying to give the kids in our communities a better shot at life. We joyfully and hopefully work at it, not regarding our efforts as a horrible burden.

Most young people accept the opportunities and go way beyond our dreams for them. Some always feel entitled to whatever they don't have. They grieve for it and grow into adults who are never satisfied, still grieving because the world does not put them center stage on its program.

As adults they are the people who can't keep a job because it's not important enough or they just can't get up and get there on time. No longer able to live with themselves and the mess they have created, they turn one last time to blaming someone else.

There is always someone with a lot of guilt and another piece of legislation, but guns or poverty or a hundred other things don't make losers. Attitude does.

The "I don't care" losers at the softball game made a choice. They chose to save themselves a lot of pain and suffering. They chose not to risk failure by simply not trying to win. As their choice revealed itself, they were soon eliminated from the game. They moved into the shade with a cold soft drink. From there they could wallow in self-pity, commiserate with their kind about the cruel world and make fun of the players still on the field.

Winners have to keep playing, keep trying. That's the rule. And that's a lot of work on a baseball field or in a rodeo arena or in life. Success doesn't come overnight. Every morning the winners have to do it again. They have to go back to work or to school or into disciplined training.

As a society I think we've given the bad attitude losers too much credit, worried about them too much. We should be laughing at their stupidity—laughing directly in their faces.

The joke is on them. They've missed the boat and—good news—it's not our fault. It's their choice.

Thankfully there are not many of them. ★

~Comments~

"When life gives you scraps, make quilts."
—Anita's e-mail

Persevere with a Smile

Jean Strong, The Independent, September 1950

PEOPLE laughed when my college friend and I said we were driving to Denver in a Crosley automobile. It was my first vacation from the newspaper. Lois is a pharmacist in Marion, and her boss let us borrow the little car used for deliveries in their pharmacy business. The command to "Fill 'er up with Ethyl" evoked smart remarks.

"Does that little hole in the fender lead to the tank?"

"It does." In fact, a Crosley's gas tank holds six gallons. At 35-miles-per-gallon we could drive a half-day without refilling.

We had arranged the interior for comfort; the copilot could stretch out full length to sleep while the other drove on. We had a thermos of lemonade and a refrigerated bag of tuna fish sandwiches.

For the Crosley we carried two gallons of water, one quart of oil, a screwdriver and a pair of pliers. What we needed, it turned out, was a rotor.

We had traveled 326 trouble-free miles that Friday and were a few miles out of South St. Joseph, Missouri when the Crosley motor sputtered, gasped and died.

After the car quit, we hailed a Missouri farmer and his wife. In less than two hours the obliging husband located the trouble, found a new rotor in St. Joseph and installed it. Bless him and the garage that was open on a Friday evening. All out of the goodness of his heart.

Two hours later, on a lonely stretch of country road, the car stalled again. It was early Saturday morning by now as we hailed two unsuspecting baseball umpires going home from a Western league game. We agreed to "tell the people back home that umpires aren't such a bad lot." So there.

When it began to rain, the umpires stopped hunting for the engine trouble and started pushing us to the town 20 miles away.

They ran out of gas while we were nine miles from Topeka. We summoned a service truck from an all-night garage. The fellow transported Lois and me and the ailing Crosley to the shop and soon had our car running again although he couldn't say what he'd done to correct the problem.

~Comments~

Doesn't everyone you meet deserve a smile in greeting? A smile, after all, is an inexpensive way to improve your looks.
—Editor's note.

Chapter 4c

Jean: "**Vacations from work** usually result in treasured memories. Among my favorites is the six-country tour of **Europe** in July 1952 when I celebrated my 27th birthday in Rome with three Iowa friends and 57 media women.

Other favorites:
In the mid-fifties Life colleague Clara Nicolai and another friend joined me for the scenic drive around the **Gaspé Peninsula, Quebec.**

In 1961, a lazy week's camping vacation in the Caribbean with my Virginia friend, Barbara Lucas, was an inexpensive recuperative break at a national park, St. John's, following a strenuous period of work in New York. We cooked our meals out-of-doors and I read *Exodus* while lolling on the beach.

Jean Strong (1952)

Perhaps a tap at a critical spot? [That worked on the 1933 Ford I drove to high school in the early 1940s when a tap on the carburetor encouraged it to start.]

We proceeded under our own power to our first destination in Junction City where Lois' sister lives. By then we realized the car needed expert care; no one in town could touch it until Monday when a new rotor of correct size would be ordered. Being stranded in Kansas appalled us. We decided immediately to go on by train and pick up the repaired Crosley on our return.

In defense of the little car, we contend that you can get a more comfortable ride in a Crosley than in a railway coach or a full-size automobile.

On an all-day 230-mile guided limousine tour from Denver we visited Pike's Peak, Garden of the Gods, Cave of the Winds, Van Briggle's pottery works, Colorado Springs and Manitou Springs.

The bus driver and a tour mate cowboy from Texas offered to take us to the horse races the following day. We accepted. The cowboy had accompanied racing horses from the famous King Ranch and we had a fun day trying to guess which horse would win.

I won't attempt to describe the beauty of Colorado because I couldn't do it justice. If you've seen it, you know what I mean. If you haven't you should plan to take your next vacation in and near the mile-high city. ★

~ Comments ~

Chapter 4c continued

Q. Anita, what was your favorite vacation?
"My trip to **Hawaii** in 1963 with my then best friend from high school. We stayed in Oahu for a week and did the usual things, such as attending a luau, visiting **Pearl Harbor** and seeing other tourist sites.

"But the most fun part was meeting two Marines who showed us the places where tourists don't go, such as a secluded lagoon with a waterfall. We were the only ones there. These two boys were really nice and fun to be with, and there were a lot of tears when it came time to say goodbye at the airport. I wrote to one for awhile but we gradually lost contact.

"My most memorable childhood vacations would be two I took with my parents to visit relatives. On one, I was walking alone when I fell in a creek and ended up screaming my lungs out while grabbing handfuls of earth on the bank to pull myself out of the water. When I turned up at the family dinner wet from the waist down, I was subjected to hoots of laughter and ridicule from my idiot cousins and a tongue-lashing from my mother because I wandered off by myself. To this day, I believe it was only by the grace of God that I didn't drown.

"On the other occasion (again alone) I picked and ate some cherries from a grove across the street from the people we were visiting in Oregon. Later, I heard the adults talking about the grove's owner having had the cherry trees sprayed with an insecticide, which caused me to follow my mother into the bedroom where I burst out crying, "I think I'm going to die!"

"When she heard my story, she laughed and said the trees were sprayed after I had been there. I never heard the end of that incident, either. But that's OK. I got even with my family with some of my columns over the years.

Control Freaks' Dilemma

Anita French, Daily Record, February 1995

"I KNOW you're a control freak, sister dear, but you're going to have to let me drive this time," said my younger brother. Chris made this remark recently as we were getting into his car.

"I'm sure I don't know what you're talking about," I replied in my best insouciant manner. "Drive whenever and however you please. Don't worry about me, I'll just huddle down here on the car floor with my eyes closed while you try to break the sound barrier."

To think that I used to change this kid's diapers and now he's telling me I'm a control freak. Go raise brothers!

But, what's the use of pretending. When it comes to control freakism, I'm the kind they write case studies about.

It's not easy being a control freak. You're the air traffic controller of life, trying to make all the little planes land when and where you want. And when they don't you fret.

That's a great word, "fret." It describes the sound that escapes between your clenched teeth when you're control freaking. I don't know where it all starts—probably in the womb. There you are, lying in that warm, dark sac, looking at your watch and fretting, "C'mon, c'mon, let's get these wagons rolling."

And when control freaks become parents, they go berserk. They want their children to be like homing pigeons so that no matter where they fly, they'll always land at home. If CF parents had their way, they'd tie honing devices to their children's ankles, and then monitor their movements.

Control freaks don't have support groups because we worry that the meetings will start without us. We have terrible dreams in which everything is out of control. Buttons won't button, clothes don't fit, your eyes can't see, and your feet won't move. Your hair and teeth fall out. Or you're walking down the street, naked as a jaybird.

The problem with control freaks is that they have too little patience and too much imagination. There is an apocryphal story told about control freaks. It goes something like this:

A man is driving down a country road at night. He passes a farmhouse but little else. When he gets a mile or so past

~ Comments ~

> *"It's forever up to me to be telling folks what they should do and they don't like it."*
> —Roberta Fulbright

Chapter 4d

Anita: "The Control Freak column engendered several comments from people who read it and also confessed to being control freaks. We laughed together which just shows again that if you take a humorous look at what some people call an undesirable trait, it's easier to live with if not overcome.

"I hatched from a family of control freaks. My mother is one and so is my younger brother. And my children will cheerfully agree that their mother is the Champion CF."

~~

Jean: "Anita admits to being a control freak; Cynthia says she is 'a recovering control freak,' adding, "I still like order in things important to me, but I've quit running the world."

Cynthia continues, "The big adventure is learning now to listen and see what's there before leaping to lead. It's very surprising the treasures we miss, the subtleties of life."

Jean: " I think of myself as being 'fiercely independent.' Perhaps the terms mean the same thing? Example: In 1945 a Marion, Iowa businessman kindly offered financial help with my college expenses. I thanked him with a polite: 'I want to do it myself.' After all, I had a marketable skill and, at twenty, an over-abundance of energy.

> Let my epitaph be:
> *Responsible for herself*

the farmhouse, his car has a flat. He gets out to fix the tire and discovers that his jack is not in the trunk. So he decides to walk back to the farmhouse to see if he can borrow one.

While walking he begins to think. What if the farmer is asleep and gets mad when I wake him up? What if he mistakes me for a burglar and calls the cops? What if he does help me but charges a thousand dollars to use his jack? What if he doesn't even have a jack?

By the time the man reaches the farmhouse, he has worked himself into such an angry state that he bangs his fist on the door as loud as he can and yells to those inside, "I didn't want to borrow your blankety-blank jack, anyway!"

We control freaks have a little prayer just for us. It goes, "God grant me the serenity to accept the things I cannot change, the courage to change the things I can and the wisdom to know the difference."

And step on it, Lord. ★

~Comments~

Chapter 4d continued

"Forever wary of relinquishing control over my own life, I never regretted that decision to 'do it myself.' I was free to join the Theta Sigma Phi travel group seven years later in 1952 because I had no college debt to repay. The fabulous **30-day European tour** for media mavens cost less than twenty-five dollars a day, including airfare from New York, transportation around Europe and most meals."

~~

Cynthia says her family didn't really take vacations because the family recreation business demanded their presence, especially during the summer when other people were at play. But that was okay with her. She suffered from carsickness as a child and as an adult "hates to fly." And she really does like to work.

A treasured day-off, she says, is a rainy day that can be spent in bed reading—an infrequent experience for her since all her critters must be fed and tended rain or shine."

~~

Q. You have written under two names?
Anita: "I wrote In A Nutshell under my former name, **Anita French**, for about five years. After I remarried, I became **Anita Creech**, the name on my Gray Matters column."

> *"Man's life is divided into two periods—in the first he sets a bad example; in the second he gives good advice. My children with one accord informed me I had reached the second period."*
> —Roberta Fulbright

Cynthia: "I've heard that we need one life to learn with, one life to live with."

~~

5. FAMILY

Holiday Hijinks
Anita French, Daily Record, December 1994

SO did you have a happy holiday? And did you spend it like I did—with a semi-dysfunctional family? I say that in semi-jest. My family is no more or no less dysfunctional than most. It's just that we're a bunch of irreverent smart alecks with an attitude.

My younger brother, Chris, and his family were here from Colorado. Chris is a paralegal, which doesn't mean he's a lawyer, he just does their research for them.

Being the parasmart-aleck that she is, my brother's wife, Jeannine, couldn't wait to tell me the latest Arkansas joke she'd heard. "What do a tornado, hurricane and divorce have in common in Arkansas? When all is said and done, someone has lost a trailer."

Now, before I hear from 115 irate Arkansans or even Arkanlawyers, let it be known right here that yours truly lives in a trailer . . . I mean, a mobile home, which is how we refer to them in our neighborhood, a kind neighbor once corrected me. I don't know the difference between the two, except I think a mobile home has a carport.

Anyway, Jeannine's remark soon turned into a discussion of all those pithy sayings you see in books or on T-shirts about how you know you're living in Arkansas when . . . blah, blah, blah.

That's when we realized that some of our family members could qualify for this list. Such as my son, who likes to keep at least one pair of new Levis on hand for special occasions. Or my Uncle Dale whose homemade wine makes you appreciate Carlo Rossi. Uncle Dale's stuff is so potent that my Dad (whom Dale, his brother, calls Buck) uses it on his garden and says it's also a good degreaser.

So we made up a few additions for that infamous Arkansas list. How do you know when you're living in Arkansas? When the men think getting dressed up means putting on a pair of unfaded jeans. Or when they sell a product called Buck and Dale that not only makes your garden grow and is the best thang since Goop, you can also "sap" it after dinner.

~ Comments ~

Chapter 5a

Q. Where do you get ideas for subject matter?
Anita: "For me, my family has been one of my biggest sources of column fodder. From the feedback received from readers, they identify with this, and I've concluded that everybody's family is dysfunctional in some way. One of the best ways to handle dysfunction is with humor, which is better than throwing up or having a nervous breakdown.

"Another subject source for me has been what goes on in this world. A columnist could almost write daily (and some do) about what happens in this cockamamie universe."

~~

I found out that, before I arrived, Chris and my parents had had an argument over whether the ceiling fan blades were turning clockwise or counter-clockwise. This profound problem, never being solved, was carried to the dining room table when Dad suggested we pass the food in a clockwise direction. "And which way would that be?" my smart-alecky brother asked.

And it was downhill from there. We soon regressed into the past, remembering when each of us took a pratfall. For Jeannine, it was when she was 18 and pridefully refused a steadying hand from one of her college professors as they walked on ice-covered stairs. Jeannine fell flat on her proud behind, causing the professor to laugh, "Remember, Jeannine, pride goeth before a fall."

Jeannine won't appreciate my repeating this story. In fact, my mother told me she was getting tired of the family being used as fodder for my columns and she's thinking of suing.

At last, a semi-legal case my brother can parahandle. ★

A Child's Western Lifestyle
Cynthia Haseloff, The Morning News, June 2000

THE pony is five times older than the child. A pee wee in the official scheme, four-year-old Dally is enjoying her first full season as a barrel racer with Chief, a handsome tolerant Paint horse.

Winning is not yet her goal. The color of ribbons interests her more than its meaning; she wants yellow and white ones along with the blues and reds. Does her mom, Angie Clark—barrel racer, trainer, and producer—see that as a problem?

"No, for now I just want Dally to have fun. Too many parents put too much pressure on their kids and make them hate the sport in the long run," says Angie.

Running the cloverleaf pattern around the barrels at events is still a privilege for this young lady. At her home in Oklahoma she must complete a run on a stick horse around barrel pillows—in the proper direction and sequence—before Chief is even loaded into the trailer for the trip to the arena. Dally is a lucky kid in many ways. When she gets up in the morning, Chief is often saddled and waiting. The pair spends a good part of the day together just riding. A lot of kids dream such a life and for Dally it's as natural as the native oaks that shade her sandbox.

Born into a family that understands the great and small issues of Western life, Dally is the fifth generation in the illustrious Veach, Beals, and Clark clan. Her father Derek is a champion saddle bronc rider who recently topped the million-dollar mark in earnings.

Her grandfather Duke, one of the finest horsemen around, also made a name riding rough stock on the rodeo circuit. Her great-grandfather, Charley Beals, was a champion bull rider. Her great-grandmother, Imogene Veach Beals, winner of the Tad Lucas Memorial Award, (presented October 2001 during the Rodeo Hall of Fame inductions at the National Cowboy and Western Heritage Museum) was a trick rider and today knows more about women's rodeo than the authors who interview her.

This family has learned there's no short cut to excellence. It's just a steady, wise journey. Angie sums up the process: "Time and good instruction are the best way to learn to ride."

As privileged as she is by birth and upbringing, Dally is not the only child growing up around the barrels. Although

~ Comments ~

Chapter 5b

Q. Cynthia, how would you characterize your column?
"EquiNotes is concerned with **horse activities** and the life style built around them. My own bias is toward the Western, naturally. In researching a future book, I got hooked on barrel racing.

"I rode English and did a little jumping years ago. I can truthfully say without modesty that I was never any good at it. But I hope, as Emily Dickinson once said, that my soul stands ajar and I am willing to credit any equine sport that involves cooperation between the human and the creature, and that does not encourage or promote cruelty or breeding for genetic faults."
~~

Five truths learned by children:
1. No matter how hard you try, you can't baptize cats.

2. When your Mom is mad at your Dad, don't let her brush your hair.

3. You can't trust dogs to watch your food.

4. You can't hide a piece of broccoli in a glass of milk.

5. The best place to be when you're sad is Grandpa's lap.
—Jean's e-mail
~~

most of these youngsters are not members of professional rodeo families, they all live in close proximity to the horse and their family.

Traveling the highways and Interstates on weekends you can see them in their pickups towing horses in trailers. Parents go to the trouble and expense for many reasons. Equine sports teach responsibility, winning and losing, joy and disappointment—all useful experiences for life.

Unlike many activities that focus on children alone and confine parents to the sidelines, equine events allow parents and kids to have a common ground where both participate actively. Parent wisdom and skills have meaning. Children can respect the knowledge and learn from it.

But mostly it's worth parental effort because they share an interest and a long ride with their children. It's a chance to be alone, seemingly focused on an activity, but truly just being together—a family uninterrupted by school or activities or business, and away from the bombardment of values not their own.

For a few hours they transcend the complications of their lives and concentrate on the basic family relationship. What could be more important? ★

~Comments~

Chapter 5b continued

Five truths learned by adults:
1. Raising teenagers is like nailing Jell-o to a tree.

2. Wrinkles don't hurt.

3. Families are like fudge . . . mostly sweet, with a few nuts.

4. Laughing is good exercise. It's like jogging on the inside.

5. Middle age is when you choose your cereal for the fiber, not the joy.
—Jean's e-mail

~~

Barrel Racing for All Ages
Cynthia Haseloff, Morning News, July 2000

E ARLY in 1999 I was spending too much time in the library researching the 19ᵀᴴ century West, and I began to feel a need to find out what was going on today in the waning 20ᵀᴴ century. Discovery began with a couple of tickets to Lady Razorback basketball games as the women vied for a national title.

Sitting in the Bud Walton Arena with the record-setting crowd, I sensed something had changed since my youth. Women were now both serious athletes and serious fans.

Before falling asleep later, I thought about this changed world and wondered if there was comparable phenomenon in the world of Western equine sports.

I asked a friend about barrel racing. A woman of my own generation, she said, "There's nothing to it. You just get on a horse and run like the devil around three barrels. That's it." She gave me the name of someone else to call that knew more and really "liked" the sport.

A few weeks later I attended my first barrel racing only event at the nearby Oak Grove Riding Club arena just off I-540. A commanding view of the Holiday Inn and Convention Center from the arena presents an interesting commingling of the hustling contemporary world with Western custom.

Arriving at the grounds, I noted a lot of trucks and trailers, not a passenger car in sight. Some of these rigs were state of the art; they looked and were very expensive. Other trailers were small two-horse wired together rusty things.

The scene was new and wonderful. All around me were women and children and horses and dogs—and a few men. Several were dads getting sons or daughters off to a good start or just fellowshipping with their families.

Equine sports offer equal opportunity to men and women. Skills—not sex or size—determine the rider's status. This is an appealing element for me.

It seemed unique, a woman's world reminiscent of my old girls' school days. Women were in the announcer's booth and served as timekeepers and entry fee collectors. Women sat on their saddled horses with children in front of them, chatting with friends under the shade of old trees. They looked as comfortable as other women do around a luncheon table.

~ Comments ~

Chapter 5c

Q. How did you get started as a columnist?
Cynthia: "Attending barrel racing events as part of my research for a contemporary western, I noticed how many families were deeply involved with horses and the **Western-Southern counter culture**. I also noticed that not much was being written about them or for them. Hence the column."

> "**Risk**: You cannot discover new oceans unless you have the courage to lose sight of the shore."
> —Cynthia's e-mail

A friend—also an animal person—and I were amazed at the easy natural camaraderie of people and horses. Competitive events were taking place, but the atmosphere did not seem stressful. It was not like a soccer game or Little League. No parents were messing up the fun.

When the children ran their ponies—and some of the kids were tiny four-year-olds—everyone in the stands shouted encouragement. "Come on, Dakota. Kick! Kick! Kick!" with a final burst of cheers and "Good ride!" as the last barrel was rounded and child and pony sprinted home down the center of the arena.

We saw what we thought was going to be a stage mother standing in the alleyway watching her child run. Yes, this young mother was shouting, but mostly she was monitoring, watching her child take a step toward independence.

We sensed the mother was not pushing. Rather she wanted to make sure the child was safe and learning properly. As the little girl and mama's big horse charged out of the arena, blasting past the calm parent, we heard mama shout a strong "Whoa" and watched the obedient old horse skid to a stop with his precious cargo.

One generation was preparing the next. A worthy pursuit, is it not? ★

Grandson to the Rescue

Jean Strong, Innisfree Newsletter, November 1999

CECIL and Iris Flack of Rogers had reason to be especially proud of their grandson, Craig, when they learned of a heroic rescue he made in mid-June 1998.

Heavy rains over the weekend had caused flooding on Mosquito Creek near Bagley in southwest Iowa. A barricade on highway 141 warned travelers of the treacherous conditions.

Craig Flack, 36, his wife Brenda, and their three children were driving around the area in their four-wheel-drive pickup that Sunday night, assessing damage to their farmlands. They had stopped at the barrier to watch the water flowing over the roadway.

Suddenly a car came from behind and swerved around the barricade. The swirling water swept the Chrysler New Yorker off the roadway into the watery ditch. Noting the danger to its driver, Flack followed with their truck until water reached the running boards. With his truck lights illuminating the disaster-in-progress, he waded and swam to the rapidly sinking car while his family watched in fear.

The woman, Annette Ahmann of Carroll, Iowa, 51, was panicking as she tried unsuccessfully to open her door against the water. Flack's efforts to kick in a window with his foot were also fruitless.

As water rose to the woman's shoulders, pressure inside the car equalized and Flack finally got the driver's door open. He pulled the woman out and up to the top of the car where both were standing when the car sank to the bottom.

"We about fell off," Flack later told reporters. "The water was above our knees. I was getting really cold so I asked, 'Can you swim?'" She said she could and they both swam to the water's edge.

The Flacks took the woman to the Bagley fire station where she hugged and thanked Flack, and asked, "How does it feel to save somebody's life?"

A friend picked up Ahmann and the Flacks returned to their home. Flack had difficulty sleeping that night. Next day he told reporters, "I'm not a hero, I'm a farmer." ★

~Comments~

Chapter 5d

Jean: "The Cecil Flacks retired in 1973 from their large restaurant and motel operation at Ankeny, Iowa. They fled Florida after four and one-half years to live in **beautiful northwest Arkansas** for their remaining retirement years.

"At **Innisfree Retirement Village** they shared an apartment with two white Maltese dogs. The small breed originated twenty-eight hundred years ago in Malta, Cecil said.

~~

Jean: "After **retiring to Arkansas** in 1990 from Washington, D.C. and Time-Life Books, I contributed to Rose Christensen's 'Reading Coach" column for the **Benton County Daily Record**, and to the newsletter at Innisfree Retirement Village in Rogers."

~~

Jean Strong's **40-year journalism career** took her from Cedar Rapids, Iowa to New York, Philadelphia and Washington, D.C. and back again.

"I was on the staff at two magazines (Life and Fortune) and two book publishers (Farm Journal and Time-Life Books), and I'm not finished yet," she says although she "chooses her own projects now."

As a **freelancer** in the 1960s she created and published three annual promotion publications for Iowa (1964 through 1966), a family genealogy (1978) and in 1996 the historical non-fiction work, *A Prairie Almanac, 1839 to 1919* based on a first-person manuscript left by a pioneer ancestor. **Jean** is currently planning and will be writing in 2002 a 100-year illustrated history of the public library in her hometown (Marion, Iowa) for publication before 2005.

~Comments~

Chapter 5d continued

Anita Creech is currently conducting interviews for a book about black families in northwest Arkansas. The book is a joint venture with **Myra Moran**, a bookseller who specializes in books about Arkansas.

Cynthia Haseloff, of course, is working between law classes on a short story and a couple of novels, as well as considering a venture in book packaging.

~~

6. COUNTRY LIVING

Food, Fellowship and Love
Anita French, Daily Record, July 1995

THE aroma of grilled hamburgers and the sound of laughter greeted me Thursday as I opened the door to the church house in Little Flock. One of the members had invited everyone to a hamburger and homemade ice cream supper, saying he would supply the food and do the cooking. We quickly took him up on his offer.

A little late, I had to catch up with those already sitting at tables, eating, talking, laughing and teasing the chef who couldn't keep the hamburgers and hot dogs coming fast enough. Four ice cream makers sat churning on the kitchen counter. They were filled with different flavors: homemade vanilla, cherry vanilla, blueberry-cheesecake and pineapple ice cream.

The pastor brought in a plate heaped with the latest grill offering, yelling over the noise that there were more hamburgers and hot dogs ready to eat. Meanwhile, he kept himself busy swatting the flies that had followed the food and now circled our plates like kamikaze pilots.

A visitor from California stopped by to chat. Someone remarked that they grew almonds up her way, didn't they. And did you know, her questioner noted, that we'uns say "aay-monds," while in California they say "all-monds?"

As we hunched over bowls of cold, sweet ice cream that hurt your teeth and added a few more inches to the waistline, the pastor interrupted by requesting everyone's attention. One of the members had something he wanted to say.

Leaning on his cane, this dear old man said in a quavering voice nearly too frail to be heard that he just wanted to let us know how much he had enjoyed this, and how much he loved everyone here. Then, putting on his cap, he headed slowly for the door before emotion got the better of him.

Quiet at first, and not knowing what else to do, we applauded as he walked away. Several people called out, "We love you too, John." Turning my attention back to the ice cream, I suddenly found it hard to swallow.

~ Comments ~

"Roberta (Fulbright) believes strongly in the power of love. She also believes in the power of work."
—Lessie Read, editor

Chapter 6a

Churches Are Plentiful
Each Saturday *The Morning News* publishes in its Religion section a directory of area churches. It is not surprising that Baptist churches are more numerous than any of the other denominations that include: Assembly of God, Catholic, Christian, Christian Science, Church of Jesus Christ of Latter Day Saints, Episcopal, Lutheran, Methodist, Nazarene, Orthodox, Pentecostal, Presbyterian, Unity and Seventh-day Adventist.

Also **Bahai centers** in Fayetteville, Rogers and Springdale; and a **Buddhist Center** and **Jewish Temple** in Fayetteville

Another 80-plus churches are listed under 'other.' They include Assembla Apostolica de la Fe en Christo Jesus in **Rogers**, Community churches in **Bella Vista** and **Lost Bridge**, the Cowboy Church of NW Arkansas and the Salvation Army both in **Springdale**, and the Religious Society of Friends (Quakers) in **Fayetteville**.

Nearly 400 churches in all are listed with the address, pastor and times of worship services in the 1 March 2002 issue.

~~

The following Sunday, as we sang a hymn, I watched as some of the women greeted the former pastor's wife who has Alzheimer's. Their faces lit in welcome, they hugged and kissed her and helped lead her to her place. One of the women, a recent widow, then returned to her seat, her eyes reddened by tears.

We all sin against our Lord in a thousand ways, every minute of the day, every day. But you take some comfort in hoping that He sees, "Behold, how they love one another!" ★

~ Comments ~

Chapter 6a continued

Greetings, Tourists
 "Every person in every pickup waves. It's called 'being friendly.' Try to understand the concept."

Enjoy your visit and then Go Home! We welcome your stopover, but the explosive population growth over the past 10 years is straining the capability of our city and county governments. Give us a break while our elected officials work on the problems.
—Editor's Note

"Arkansans started hunting and fishing when they were nine years old. 'Yes, we saw Bambi.' they will tell you. 'We got over it.' "
—Internet.

Love Is a Multi Splendored Thing

Cynthia Haseloff, Morning News, June 2000

ANTICIPATION and enjoyment have given way to memory and meditation—like the day after Christmas. Pat Parelli, his teams of people and horses have come and gone, leaving memories and thoughts to last through the months ahead.

Love, Language and Leadership are the keys to a good relationship between man and horse, Parelli said. Who could doubt the master? He sat on his quiet pony without bridle, walking about the arena classroom, the horse responding to his unspoken commands.

Parelli told all of us—and we nodded our heads in agreement—that some people love horses. It isn't a convenient emotion but some of us have it. We love to see horses, to touch horses. We love to be with horses.

We absolutely love horses so much that we love to smell horses. We take secret sniffs whenever we have the chance. He said that is the ultimate test for true love. Horses always smell good. We love these creatures.

We also know these beloved horses have faults, some small and annoying, some truly dangerous. Horses shy at tiny pieces of paper. They open gates that would stop Houdini. They won't stand tied. They won't pick up their feet to be cleaned. They won't load. They won't cross water a centimeter deep. Given an opportunity they are pigs. They are fearful of other horses or aggressive. They are lazy.

We know these faults and still dote on these creatures, taking what we can get, triumphing in the smallest successes. Why can we make this leap of faith with horses, but can't with the people we love?

With people we dwell on the faults, major or minor. Too often we forget that we love this other. Parents and partners are especially bad about this forgetfulness. Why is that?

Perhaps our problem lies in our shared humanness. We lack the separation, become confused by who we are and who they are and forget that they are not we and we are not they. We lose the mystery that we have with horses.

~ Comments ~

Chapter 6b

Q. You have said the clamor from revolutions (sexual, moral, technological and scientific) has grown wearisome in recent decades. Do you see hope for improvement?
Cynthia: "The past twenty years have also spawned a quiet revolution in the world of horses, thanks to some 'cowboys' who brought to light a positive human-horse relationship that existed many years ago.

"A Greek horseman, Xenophon—born four hundred years before Christ—practiced the art, and American cowboys have reintroduced it. Using their own observations and consciences, they promote a way of training horse and rider that eliminates the brutality of 2000 years.

"In the beginning, there were just a few of these '**cowboys**'—Ray Hunt, Tom and Bill Dorance—performing miracles. And they were miracles—a green colt transformed in hours into a useful companion and worker without brutality, without 'breaking'. '**Horse whisperer**' is a term these men don't like, but it expresses the sense of ancient mystery.

"Yes, there would be many hours of follow-up training, but the beginning was gentle and so effective that those who saw knew they had seen a miracle. I've observed the training several times since I first saw **Sam Powell** take a green colt to the point where its owner could ride it from the pen. I've witnessed the yielding with the horse lowering his head, licking his lips, turning in, joining up, and accepting a human to be trusted as the head of his herd.

~~

A horse never threatens our self-concept as people do. We don't think we are bad or good, worthy or unworthy, successes or failures because our horses choose to graze instead of gaze into our eyes.

Our children and spouses threaten us with sloppy habits, poor grades, disinterest, or even with the activities they pursue that don't include us. We put on them all our expectations for our own lives. Perhaps that's why we fail painfully with those we love. Yet, Parelli says, love is the basis for whatever we do successfully.

We each ultimately are just ourselves, touching other lives successfully or poorly. We can teach and encourage our children, but we cannot decide for them. We cannot be them. We cannot live through them.

If a spouse strays or leaves, we must see—as they must see—that they left because of who they are, because of their needs, not because of someone else's deficits.

People do what they do because of who they are, just as a horse shies because it is a horse—not because of the rider.

Difference, acceptance, and adjustment keep us in love with horses. Can people stay in love with each other and with their children the same way? Bridging the distance becomes an ongoing adventure and privilege. ★

~ Comments ~

Chapter 6b continued

"I used this idea for **a scene**, between the Indian Chief Satanta and the white woman Adrianne, **in Satanta's Woman**:

Satanta said, "Take my hand, I will show you wild horses as the Kiowa sees them." Pointing to the herd he says, "See over there. That is the boss."

"But the stallion is over there."

"The stallion is not the boss," confided Satanta. "He is the progenitor in season and the protector always. He guards the mares and colts from predators, but also from other stallions. He is never in the herd, always on the edge. That full-bellied bay mare is wise and wonderful. She knows things. She finds good grass and clean water. She disciplines the colts and the foolish by driving them away from the safety of the herd. She holds them away with her undaunted eye. They are very afraid because, without the herd she holds, they will be prey to the wolves. They watch her eye for any wavering. They paw and toss their heads and walk with their chins on the ground. And finally, when they are humble, she takes away her hard gaze. She releases them and lets them return. She welcomes them and grooms them affectionately. They are grateful. It is the way of the wild horses."
— From Chapter 18, *Satanta's Woman.*

~~

Cassville in Missouri Turns 150
Anita French, Daily Record, July 1995

As America was celebrating another birthday this past Fourth of July a little town in Missouri was noting its sesquicentennial. Cassville, population 2,371, turned 150 years old.

Located about 35 miles northeast of the Arkansas state line, this small farming community held parades, concerts, square dances, arts and crafts, carnival rides, chicken barbecues, gospel singing and hot-air balloon races over the weekend.

A friend and I happened to wander into the tail end of Saturday's celebration and were as welcomed as if we had been expected. Picking up a local newspaper, I noted that most of the events had taken place already. A resident, hearing my comment, said, "The balloons will be taking off in just a few minutes. You don't want to miss that."

As we came out of the store, I noticed a large red object hovering just beneath some treetops and, suddenly, it rose— up, up and away. Five more followed almost immediately. They were red and green, red and blue, red and yellow and one of them had big black horses painted on the side. The race was on, destination a field about 15 miles outside of town.

Wandering around we came into the town square where microphones were being put away, signs taken down and tables folded up. The crafts and music shows were over.

We passed by a three-story white house that was decorated with American flags, red, white and blue ribbons fluttering in the breeze and patriotic bunting draped over the porch railings. Built in the 1800s, the house looked like it was waiting for President Lincoln to step out onto the upstairs balcony to address the cheering crowd below.

Driving away we got behind the caravan that was following the balloons. Five balloons were still in the air, descending quickly as they neared the landing field. The long caravan turned left off the highway, on its way to welcome them all and cheer the winner.

Cassville was a friendly town. People waved at you from sidewalks, porches and cars. An editorial in the local newspaper, The _Cassville Democrat_ ("Continuing to Cover

~ Comments ~

> _"Our taxes, our crops, our battles, our celebrations, our resorts and our interests are one and the same . . . change is constant and business institutions must grow or die. We specialize in growing."_
> —Roberta Fulbright, 1937

Chapter 6c

Spring and fall **craft fairs** are rife throughout our area. Crafters from many states gather to sell their creations, and visitors return year after year to enjoy the fun of shopping in **Bella Vista**, **Bentonville**, **Rogers**, **War Eagle** and at smaller fairs in between.

~~

Bentonville, Arkansas launched its annual **Ozark Balloon Fest** in the year 2000 in early May.

~~

Ride in a Balloon Recalled
Jean: "I was between jobs and my mother had died in 1978. Friends in Madison, New Jersey invited me (from D.C.) for the weekend with a birthday surprise in mind. We would get up at 4 A.M. to make a phone call and learn whether the Big Surprise would take place, they said. Turned out it would.

"We four were on the road an hour later. My first inkling of their intent dawned as we arrived at a field where several balloons were being readied for flight. The air was calm, a requirement for these free flights in which the wind takes you and the balloon where it will.

"Marcia and her 89-year-old mother were first up in our balloon while Barbara and I followed in the chase car, and listened to the conversations with the pilot who did his best to predict their landing place. After several attempts the basket finally touched down in a farmyard and startled a farmer at his chores. Nonetheless, he obligingly held the rope dangling from the basket.

"Breathless from our run between the car and barnyard, Barbara and I

Barry County Like the Morning Dew"), listed 10 things the editor liked best about living there. Among them were: people still wave to each other when they meet on the street, city council meetings and football games begin with a prayer, and Cassville schools celebrate "Trout Day" by letting children out of school to fish at nearby Roaring River State Park.

I wouldn't have been a bit surprised to see Andy Taylor and Opie walking down a country road on their way to the fishing hole.

In 1893 the town was destroyed by fire and the citizens rebuilt it. In 1896 the townspeople built a railroad from Cassville to Exeter, so that Cassville wouldn't be left behind, the editor wrote.

As I sat outside on that July 4th night, listening to the fireworks, I thought about Cassville, the little town that didn't want to be left behind. In many ways, it is 150 years removed from life in the city. Of course, it has some of the same problems. But the nice thing about a Cassville, Missouri is that you know you can go home again, now and then. ★

~ Comments ~

Chapter 6c continued

helped our predecessors out, and climbed into the basket. Off we soared over cow and horse pastures. Our pilot was good at people and animal relations; he evaded a stampede by speaking to the animals before whooshing more gas into the balloon to adjust altitude. A half-hour later we landed in a schoolyard near New Hope, Pennsylvania.

"After helping the two pilots (husband and wife) collapse and crank the balloon into its carrier, we six enjoyed a bottle of champagne from a wicker hamper served in proper glasses on a red-and-white tablecloth. Then we drove to a nearby restaurant for a convivial breakfast. It was great fun for all and, for me an unforgettable **53rd birthday**. I recommend it as a very special treat.

Q. Anita, you live in the city but obviously enjoy country things.
"Yes, I do, especially the people. I once thought to myself that if I had a choice between attending a cocktail party where the best and brightest were or going to a **pie supper**, I'd choose the latter in an Arkansas minute.

"In fact, I attended my first pie supper just a few years ago, where pies were actually auctioned off—some as high as $150—to raise money for restoring an old school that had seen better days. It was one of the most enjoyable events I've ever attended—again mainly because of the people. No pretensions. No glamour. Just down-home hospitality and friendship. It is one of my fondest memories."
~~
Cynthia: "My dad was active in Chamber of Commerce work. This and his business took our family to many rural schools and churches for pie suppers. The food was really good: real fried chicken and home canned green beans. My dad was a marvel to all because he ate the pie first. This was more a function of timing than appetite. The organizers put out the pie first."

Cowboy Christmas Is a Tradition

Cynthia Haseloff, Morning News, July 2000

RODEO, of course, grew from the activities of working ranch hands in the West, but got its official start through the packaging and promotional skills of Colonel William F. Cody.

"Buffalo Bill" Cody is world-famous for his Wild West Shows, but on the Fourth of July 1882 in North Platte, Nebraska, he created an event that became known as "Cowboy Christmas."

This period around the Fourth now sees cowboys and cowgirls hauling all over the country for a marathon of rodeos with points and cash winnings as their goals.

Many who come to the Professional Rodeo Cowboy Association event in Springdale make one ride, or run, before heading out to compete in other rodeos across the country. When they win, it is Cowboy Christmas indeed.

During its half century of existence the Springdale rodeo has attracted many renowned cowboys—rodeo names like Fred Whitfield, Jim Shoulders, Casey Tibbs, Jim Bynum, Todd Whatley, Bennie Combs, Freckles Brown. And new champions continue to attend.

In June of 1945 a caravan of Northwest Arkansas citizens set out to advertise the new July event. These caravans were an annual prolog to the rodeo for many years. They were fun too.

Everyone donned western attire. The "squaw dress" was a popular item with the ladies. My mother had a white one with a full tiered skirt and lots of red rickrack. In my child's eyes she was especially beautiful in that dress.

Many riding club members trucked their horses from town to town to participate in the promotion. As the line of honking automobiles and waving occupants rolled into towns along the route, the announcer—often my dad because he had a public address system—invited bystanders to the coming Springdale event. We were careful, of course, not to make noise around the hospitals.

As I recall there was usually a flatbed trailer, quickly converted into a stage on any downtown street. The Skunk Holler Hillbilly Band, headed by P.W. "Doc" Boone and later by Joe Robinson, with historian D. D. Deaver playing the

~ Comments ~

Chapter 6d

Northwest Arkansas enjoys a strong **industrial base** of companies known nationally and internationally, and they are important to our state's economy. **Bentonville** hosts headquarters for the **world's largest retail merchant** (WalMart). Two of **Springdale's** early rodeo leaders, Harvey Jones and John Tyson, founded companies of national prominence in trucking and poultry processing. In 2001 Tyson's acquired Iowa Beef Packers. IBP had led the revolution in meat processing in the 1960s. Tyson's is now the **largest meat processing company in the world** (poultry, beef and pork).

Bentonville, Arkansas is the largest of seven U.S. communities named Bentonville. The other Bentonvilles range in size from zero population to a few hundred and are scattered westward from North Carolina and Virginia to Ohio, Indiana, Missouri and Texas.
—*Daily Record*, August 1999

~~

Jean: "Arkansas settlers in the early days migrated from Missouri to Northwest Arkansas because the plateaus of the Ozarks provided a cooler climate and good scenery. In 1990 those two attractions, and the friendliness of the people, encouraged me to move here from Washington, DC."

~~

jug, entertained with blue grass music and a comedy review while pitching the rodeo.

These old rodeo caravans created a lot of good feeling before moving on to the next town. The junket—arduous before air-conditioning came to automobiles—began early and lasted late into the June twilight. Everyone who made the trek was tuckered out from all the good spirits and enthusiasm.

It was show business after all, so everyone had put his best foot forward for the event and the hometown. That's a lot of work on any day. ★

7. FOOD AND EATING

Which Way to the Kitchen?

Anita French, Daily Record, August 1995

PASSING a home that had a barbecue grill in the front yard, a friend remarked to me that it was odd how it's usually men who want to do the outdoor cooking. "They burn five dollars worth of meat . . . nothing's said. But let the wife burn something in the kitchen and it's a big deal."

It is strange how we've appointed men as the backyard chefs. Must have something to do with it being the robust, big-shouldered, great outdoors.

After all, most outdoor cooking is done either on a patio or the lawn where there are masculine things such as wood chips, gravel, mulch or cement. In the kitchen, on the other hand, there are shiny, waxed floors, curtains with daisies on them and little blenders that whir.

Frankly, I've never understood the cooking mystique whether indoors or out. As a family chef, I was mediocre at best. Part of it was my natural abhorrence of cooking anything that took longer than 15 minutes, but another part of it was due to my family's innate suspicion of any dish that was "new." By new, I mean if it had some name other than "meat and potatoes."

Actually, the hubby was the beef and spud person. He probably got that way after trying to eat the first meal I ever cooked as a newlywed. It was chicken, peas, and something. Wanting to get the chicken crisp "just like mom's," I turned up the flame under the skillet and fried a whole chicken in less than 30 minutes. It was a colorful chicken—dark golden brown on the outside and bright pink on the inside.

The frozen peas added a nice touch. Bright green they were, just like they came out of the package. That's because they were just like they came out of the package. When hubby tried to put a fork in them, they boinged up into the ceiling. Meanwhile, yours truly boo-hooed in the kitchen.

Those early days were not tidings of better meals to come. There was still the "children's hour" to go through, or A Thousand and One Nights of Hamburgers, Hot Dogs and

~ Comments ~

"The older you get the tougher it is to lose weight because, by then, your body and your fat are really good friends."
—Anita's e-mail

Chapter 7a

Anita: "As you can see from my picture, I love both food and eating. Except, sometimes I think the only reason I was born was so I could spend my life trying to lose weight."

~~

Tacos, as I call it. There's nothing like two teenagers with pizza sauce in their blood, and a husband who grunts "Where's the beef?" to kill any culinary creativity.

I also went through the "earth mother" phase, making our own bread and canning vegetables. Home economists say you save money doing this but I don't believe a syllable of it. Home-baked bread disappears faster than you can say Wonder Years, and you end up baking six more loaves at midnight and going into debt.

As for home gardens, we grew one three years in a row. I knew it was time to stop when the six cases of pickled okra that I canned had to be hauled off during the city's big items trash day.

My evening meals now usually consist of whatever comes out of a can or package. Once in awhile I find myself admiring a picture of some food dish, until I look at the ingredients and see it calls for something like dried alligator tongue from Zanzibar. Then I fondly recall my days with Betty Crocker, Campbell Soup and Kraft Macaroni Dinners.

That's why I became a writer. ★

A Guide to Good Ribs

Cynthia Haseloff, Morning News, May 2000

AFTER several months in hot pursuit of the perfect rib I can report: There is a shortage. Why is this? Are new customers over-burdening the old rib infrastructure? Or do a majority of new customers lack information about what a good rib should be?

Real ribs are primarily pork or beef. Pigeon and hummingbird ribs have proven less satisfactory. The pre-formed sops for sauce that appear from time to time in fast food chains are not ribs.

Most connoisseurs prefer the meatier, tenderer pork ribs. If you are a bone gnawer, pork ribs allow for satisfactory gnawing. If you are a gristle eater, baby back ribs are the way to go.

Real ribs don't float. Too much grease on your plate reveals ribs improperly cooked and wallowing in grease. Feel nauseous after eating ribs? That's a dead giveaway.

Folk who believe that beer is an industrial strength grease cutter and use it liberally—while cooking or eating ribs—don't love ribs.

Real ribs are fresh. Grocery stores sometimes sell pre-cooked ribs in their delis; some are good ribs, some aren't. If the ribs in refrigerated units are laminated, so bonded with the packaging that you can only remove them sequentially, don't buy them. They won't taste like ribs.

Some stores try to save meat that is going bad by cooking it and layering it with sauce. Getting there in time is the key to success here, but under all the embellishments, it's still bad meat. You can taste that. Know your store. If you get rotten meat, take it back.

Real ribs are tender, yield gently to the teeth, and fall moist and satisfying onto the tongue and palate. We recently anticipated eating a rack of pork ribs. Like beasts we carried them from the rib place back to our den, and struggled to tear the meat from the bones. One bite and we knew these ribs had been rushed. Is there a greater food sacrilege?

~ Comments ~

Chapter 7b

Cynthia: "The **ribs** column generated a number of comments, many in agreement. But some people out there are cooking ribs and know what they are doing.

"I have learned that when buying ribs, those with wide bones are cheaper than those with narrower bones. Country-style ribs have been deboned for those who want no bones in their ribs.

"Beef ribs will break your teeth—and your dog's. If you are a gristle eater, baby back ribs are the way to go.

~~

Q. What are your favorite foods, and restaurant?
Anita: "I love Mexican and Chinese food, but for good down-home flavor you can't beat **pinto beans cooked with ham** and served with yellow cornbread. It's Arkansas caviar, Ozark ambrosia and food of the lesser gods.

"I really don't have a favorite restaurant. The only place I make a point of visiting often is The Market at Pinnacle Point, **Rogers**, because of it's a la carte and gourmet dessert items. It's a good place to have a delicious lunch while reading a book. You are reading a book or something, aren't you?"

~~

Jean: "I love the **grilled Cajun catfish** served at the Dixie Café near I-540 between **Rogers** and **Bentonville**. Several area restaurants serve excellent farm-raised fried catfish with hush puppies and fries, but grilled catfish are a healthier choice. Another plus is that Dixie Café offers a light menu for those with smaller appetites, featuring half portions of the entree with generous portions of the vegetables and side dishes. You can select from a long list of main and side dishes that taste like home cooking to me. They also offer fried catfish for those who prefer that."

I've always thought rib cooks were a cut above the mundane chef, people who enjoy their art, take their time perfecting the succulent morsels. Facing facts, I fear rib guys are selling out.

Pork ribs must be fully cooked. Remember the little trichinosis worms from your school text? The laws of thorough cooking have not been repealed. Serving raw pork ribs reveals greed and lack of concern for the patron. If this rib joint gets sued, they deserve it.

Real ribs are not burned. Is this woman never satisfied? Hates raw ribs; now hates cooked ribs. Rib preparation is an art. So-called "blackened" ribs are burned on the outside and raw in the middle. Burned food, according to the latest and best information, is carcinogenic. We want ribs not cancer.

Real ribs taste good. Sauce is a garnish, not a cover-up. Forty-eleven brands of barbecue sauce are sold. Every single label testifies that the product within is the best. Don't believe it.

Here are some **tips.** Good sauce should be thicker rather than thin—simply because it sticks to the ribs better and doesn't run off. The other ingredients will be a subjective blend of tomatoes, garlic, onions, and other mysterious herbs and spices, including possibly red pepper and vinegar.

Current emphasis is placed on mesquite smoke in cooking ribs. A born Texan knows that mesquite stinks—too much of it ruins the taste.

Confer with your rib joint chef. Come to a mutual understanding of what makes good ribs. Demand the best. It's your heritage—protect it. ★

~ Comments ~

Chapter 7b continued

Anita and Jean like to eat but are not fond of cooking, Cynthia enjoys it when she has time. She also likes fast food like Junior Sonic Burgers, Taco Bell chalupas and pizza from the Hut.

For a special treat she favors carryout from Mama Z's in **Tonitown**, an Italian settlement that celebrates an annual Grape Fest. Cynthia and her dad like the **homemade spaghetti, fried chicken**, great salad and **pie** (especially coconut) from Mama Z's.

~~

**You'll never hear
a TRUE Southerner say:**

"Trim the fat off that steak."

"I'll have grapefruit instead of biscuits and gravy."

"I'll have the arugula and radicchio salad."

"I believe you cooked those green beans too long."

"Would you like your fish poached or broiled?"

"Bring my salad dressing on the side."

"Give me the small bag of pork rinds."

"We're vegetarians."

—Cynthia's e-mail

How the Café Got Its Name

Jean Strong, The Independent, January 1950

WHEN one sees old friends on the University of Iowa campus, they ask, either out of politeness or curiosity, "What are you doing now and where are you?"

I tell them I'm in Center Point and they reply, "Oh, yes, that café on the highway with the funny name. It's called Whistlestop or something like that?"

That's my cue to say, "You mean the This'L-Do Café on Highway 151."

I have ceased to be amazed when people associate Center Point with the café. The other day I asked owner Louie Pech how he happened to hang that name on his establishment. As a matter of fact, he didn't actually intend to call it "This'L-Do."

A mistake was made, albeit fortuitous, when the license for operation was made out and the "Thistledew Café" became and has remained the This'L-Do. ★

~ Comments ~

"The nice part about living in a small town is that when you don't know what you're doing, someone else does."
—Anita's e-mail

Chapter 7c

Cynthia tells about a luncheon with friends, both chic and powerful in business.

"While eating the dinner that I'd prepared, one said she could not cook. Amazing, thought I, what does she eat?

"The other table guest supplied the answer to my unspoken question by telling us of a new restaurant to avoid. 'Everything on its menu comes from Sam's. My heavens,' she added, 'I can get that at home.'

"Real women eat out for home cooking," Cynthia observed.

~~

~Comments~

Chapter 7c continued

Jean: "In the fall of 1950 I **returned to the university campus** to finish work on my liberal arts degree. It was an anti-climax after a year of turning out the weekly newspaper in Center Point, but in February of 1951 I was among the large group (500+) of mid-year graduates receiving a college diploma.

A young family friend in attendance later described the scene as a waiting exercise—waiting for the one person she knew among the hundreds of strangers marching across the stage. It seemed like that to me also. My close friends had graduated in 1948 and 1949." I did know several of the university officials on the stage and that helped.

Speaker for the occasion was a professor who delivered one of his classroom lectures. I was happy that I'd not taken any of his classes.

~~

8.   The Language

A Word to the Wise

Arkansas Press Association, Award Winner
Anita French, Daily Record, June 1994

LET scientists peer through telescopes and gaze in wonder at black holes in space. And let philosophers ponder the mysteries of the universe. What I want to know is, who took the "ugh" out of doughnut? What's more, who gave them permission?

I've had it with the donuts, nites, lites, thrus and BBQs of this world. You don't get to make up your own spelling of words. This is the English language and there are rules, people.

Granted, the rules are arbitrary and Byzantine, and were probably thought up by linguists and grammarians who moonlighted as rack operators during the Inquisition. They may be silly rules, but they're our rules.

It was one thing to see "donuts" on a place that sold them. You could excuse that, even if you didn't like it, because there's only so much room on a sign. I figured another reason they took the "ugh" out of doughnuts is because that's how you feel after eating one of those cellulite stealth bombs.

It's also what you say when you spot your backside in the mirror and see those "donuts" hanging on your thighs. That's where you should have applied them directly in the first place.

But when "donuts" started showing up in school menus, I knew Armageddon was just around the corner. School is where teachers live, for Pete's sake. When I was in school, taking liberties with the English language made teachers either gasp, shudder or close their eyes in pain as if you had dangled a participle under their nose.

And what's with all this "lite" stuff? Walking through a grocery store these days is like taking a trip through the lite fantastic. Lite mayonnaise. Lite cheese. Lite snacks. Lite brownies. Who wants a lite brownie, for crying out loud? That's like asking for a healthy hot dog.

Frankly (no bun intended), I think the people behind all this unbearable liteness of being should be sentenced to some heavy reading—Shakespeare, for instance. Can you imagine him writing, "But soft what lite thru yonder window breaks?

To Pun Is Human

A bicycle can't stand on its own because it is two-tired.

You feel stuck with your debt if you can't budget.

He had a photographic memory that was never developed.

Those who get too big for their britches will be exposed in the end.

Santa's helpers are subordinate clauses.
—Jean's e-mail

. . . Good nite, Good nite. Parting is such sweet sorrow, That I shall say good nite till it be morrow." Fie! Good thing old Will didn't have to suffer the slings and arrows of outrageous spelling.

Included in this list of heretics are city officials who have put up "not a thru street" signs all over the kingdom. I know, I know, "thru" is listed in the dictionary, but so are a lot of other four-letter words that are just as unacceptable in civilized intercourse.

Of course, city planners and such are notorious for their "oversite" of such mundane things as correct spellings of streets and so forth. One city to the west of us has been misspelling Lake Francis for so long that the woman it's named for, Frances, has given up in despair and probably thought of changing her own name. And let's not forget the unkindest cut of all—'Shakespear' Drive in Bella Vista.

At least these are unintentional errors, unlike those who want our children to go thru life thinking they have to turn on the lite so they can see in the nite. Would someone please turn out that lite?

Enuf is enuf. ★

~ Comments ~

Chapter 8a continued

General Self-editing Tips

Pronouns
"Make sure each pronoun agrees with <u>their</u> antecedent.

"Just between you and <u>I</u>, the case of pronouns is important."

"Don't use <u>no</u> double negatives. Like we just did."

"A writer must not shift <u>your</u> point of view. [Writer is singular his or her.]

"About sentence fragments. I like them when appropriate to saying what one means."

Commas:
"In letters essays and reports use commas to separate items in a series. Like we just didn't for 'letters, essays and reports."

"Check to see if you any words out."

Wordiness:
"In my opinion, I think that <u>an author</u> when he is writing <u>should</u> definitely <u>not</u> get into the habit of making <u>use</u> of too many unnecessary <u>words</u> that <u>he does not</u> really <u>need</u> in order <u>to put his message across</u>."

"Consult the <u>dictionery</u> to avoid <u>mispelings</u>.

"Last but not least, lay off clichés."

List originally compiled by George L. Trigg.

—Anita's e-mail

Barrel-racing Terminology

Cynthia Haseloff, Morning News, July 2000?

KNOWING the vocabulary can enhance your enjoyment of barrel racing. Basic terms are jackpot, exhibition and 4-D in this fast-growing sport where speed is important to winning.

The "jackpot" is the foundation event of barrel racing—and it is a race, not a prize.

Before making jackpot runs at barrel racing events, inexperienced horses and riders have an opportunity to warm-up and become acquainted with the arena and the crowd. This trial run, which usually costs fewer than five dollars to enter, is called an "exhibition." Seasoned horses and riders rarely exhibition—especially not at top speed.

Barrel racing is about speed. To say the times are fast and the competition tight is an understatement. I've read that a horse breathes about once every eighteen seconds; a good barrel run is made in less than that.

Think of it, horse and rider circle or wrap three barrels, changing leads (the foot that will be on the inside or lead at the barrel) as they move from one to the next and, then, sprint down a good piece of dirt for home in less than 18 seconds. Eighteen seconds is mostly slow.

Local and regional barrel racing clubs sponsor 4-D jackpot events. A 4-D jackpot has four divisions. The first division—1D—determines all the others. Increments of time—usually .500 of a second—are added to the fastest time in the 1D.

Thus the 2D is the fastest time in the 1D plus .500 of a second. Three-D adds a full second and 4D an entire second and a half.

A great deal of training and skill goes into putting the horse in the right position to make a smooth, quick, clean turn around each of three barrels. A rider must pick the correct spot for the horse to "rate" or set and gather his backend under himself to complete the turn and fire off that barrel toward the next.

An experienced horse at barrel racing will pick his own spot. Getting this wrong means lost time. Knocking over a barrel adds 5 seconds to a rider's time—a virtual elimination in serious competition. It can also bust knees and shins.

~ Comments ~

"Talent isn't enough. You need motivation—and persistence, too, what Steinbeck called a blend of faith and arrogance." — **Leon Uris**, Jade Walker's "The Written Word Ezine"

Chapter 8b

Cynthia: "The **4-D concept** in barrel racing grew out of the need to give many riders, not merely the very best, a chance to win. Riders pay an entry fee and draw for their place among the runners. The condition of the dirt around the barrels will affect the time of the run, so it is a matter of fairness to order the runners by chance of the draw. After several runs a tractor and rig drag the arena, leveling the playing field."

~~

The Washington Post asked its readers to assign a gender to nouns of their choice and explain their reason. VOICES selected the 'best submissions' from those listed on the Internet.

Male Nouns
HAMMER because it hasn't evolved much over the last 5,000 years, but it's handy to have around.

HOT AIR BALLOON because to get it to go anywhere you have to light a fire under it...and, of course, there's the hot air part.

SHOE because it is usually unpolished, with its tongue hanging out.

SUBWAY because it uses the same old lines to pick people up.

SWISS ARMY KNIFE because even though it appears useful for a wide variety of work, it spends most of its time just opening bottles.

~~

When barrel racers talk about their pockets, they are not referring to the ones in their jeans. For them a pocket is the safe zone around the barrel that lets them make a fast clean turn.

Barrel racers, unlike most other amateur equine competitors, don't win ribbons or trophies. They win money. Who could not like this sport? Entrants pay a fee; local club fees are $20 or less. At the end of the race, the winners split that money, and any added money from sponsors, with the club or producer.

The "filthy lucre" aspect of barrel racing may revolt some purists. But think about the good sense here. A barrel racer can theoretically actually win enough to pay for horse feed and hauling (trailering) the horse from event to event and home.

Money is a practical prize for the rider and horse that perform on that day and in that few seconds better than others. To win consistently takes wisdom, persistence, discipline, training and skill. A little luck never hurts, but it isn't required. ★

~Comments~

Chapter 8b continued

TIRE because it goes bald and often is over-inflated.

ZIPLOC BAGS because they hold everything in, but you can always see right through them.

Female Nouns
COPIER because once turned off, it takes a while to warm up. Because it is an effective reproductive device when the right buttons are pushed. Because it can wreak havoc when the wrong buttons are pushed.

HOURGLASS because over time the weight shifts to the bottom.

KIDNEYS because they always go to the bathroom in pairs.

REMOTE CONTROL [Ha! you thought I'd say male. But consider. It gives man pleasure, he'd be lost without it, and while he doesn't always know the right buttons to push, he keeps trying.]

SPONGES because they are soft and squeezable and retain water.

WEB PAGE because it is always getting hit on.
—Anita's e-mail

~~

Teen Talk in the Fifties
Jean Strong, The Cedar Rapids Gazette, May 1951

LOVE, Security, Recognition and Adventure are four things that every youngster should receive from his home and community.

Recognition is the contribution that Teen Talk is privileged to make. Beginning this week and for the next three columns, two teenagers from each of the city's high schools will be recognized for their ability to combine a part-time job with their high school work.

Too often adults underestimate the capabilities of teenagers. But on the other hand, teenagers must accept the challenge and show adults that they are capable and willing to assume responsibilities.

While much of the initiative for getting a job does lie with the individual student, he or she can get help from the school counselors or from the school system's coordinator of work experiences. The eight teenagers to be featured were selected from among those suggested by counselors from the four schools. Each student will be photographed at her or his place of work.

Seventeen-year-old Nancy Ellingson works 12 to 16 hours each week at the Northwestern Bell Telephone Company; after graduation in June she plans to continue working full-time as an operator. Now she works every other night, every other Saturday and every third Sunday. She received initial training when she began work last December, and is now in "point to point" training in which she learns to complete calls that weren't completed on the first attempt.

Nancy is one of about 45 girl students working part-time at the telephone company, an employment practice that began in 1941. Once as many as 60 high school girls were in training.

Although Nancy's free time is limited by her work and studies, she does find time to date and participate in school activities. She is a member of the executive board of the Franklin pep club, secretary for the 12A's (senior class), president of the French club and member of the Senate student government group.

Nancy likes the feeling of independence she gets from earning her own money.

~Comments~

Chapter 8c

Book Defines 'Style'
Jean: My journalism instructors at the University of Iowa in the late 1940s introduced William Strunk (1869-1946) and his take on the **Elements of Style**. My present volume of that book (Macmillan, 1979) was co-authored by **William Strunk, Jr.** and **E.B. White** who added a fifth chapter.

"The four basic chapters discuss
1. Rules of usage
2. Principles of composition
3. Matters of form
4. Commonly misused words and
   expressions.

"In the fourth chapter titled "**An Approach to Style**," White observes that 'every writer, by the way he uses the language, reveals something of his spirit, his habits, his capabilities, his bias.'

"This 'little book' is updated and published periodically to stay current. **Every writer should have a copy and use it as a reminder for improving.**"
~~
Jean: "At the *Cedar Rapids Gazette* (1951-1954), I wrote and illustrated feature articles and a weekly column for and about teenagers. It was one of many assignments. The Gazette provided a Speed Graphic camera, sheet film, flash bulbs, slave electronic flash units and tripods. I was the lone female photographer among 10 men and recall those days among my happiest at work. Two of the photographers developed film and made prints for the rest of us. In photography class we had learned to do that and it was fun. However, I found taking pictures, interviewing and writing captions and articles made more than a full week for me without adding darkroom duty.

Jim Hepner, 18, is a hospital aide at St. Luke's Hospital where he does general nursing every Saturday. "I plan to enter pre-medical training at the University of Iowa this fall and I wanted to see if I like hospital work," he said.

The six-foot student plays football and basketball but dropped football after he began working at the hospital. He is an Eagle Scout. In school he is an alternate in the Senate, member of the hospitality and the Martha Washington room committees, and tuba player in both regular and pep band.

A member of the naval reserve, he plans to undergo two weeks of training duty at Great Lakes this summer after which he will work at Camp Wapsi Y as a cabin leader and truck driver.

WHAT STUDENTS NEED in the world today, said Dr. Frank Slutz at a recent youth conference in Cedar Rapids:

1. A chance to know adults in whose integrity they can believe. Youth are beginning to wonder if we have any honest adults left in this world.

2. Some adult to whom they can talk and whose advice they respect.

3. Need to have own particular brand of intelligence recognized. Each of us is talented in certain fields. Some of us are good with our brains and some with our hands. We must be helped to develop our own particular talents.

4. A share in making the policies for the groups in which they belong—home, school, church, the gang.

5. A chance to understand the difference between morals and customs.

6. A religion they can understand and put into practice— good will for others and faith in God. ★

~ Comments ~

Chapter 8c continued

Gazette circulation exceeded 60,000 and 'Gazetteland' in the Fifties extended west from the Mississippi River over some 20 counties in eastern Iowa.

Speed Graphics were standard newspaper cameras before 35mm models, used by magazines, spread to my newspaper world.

~~

In 1954 Jean joined the LIFE magazine staff in **New York City** as a reporter. After six years at the picture magazine, she transferred to a sister magazine, *Fortune*, the business monthly, "to get back into the word business." After two years on that magazine she asked for and was granted a leave of absence to check out the truth in the adage that 'you can't go home again.'

"I did and remained in Iowa for nine years before another challenging opportunity in the East beckoned. Farm Journal's newly formed books' division in **Philadelphia** needed someone with both writing and publishing experience to shepherd some 36 books through production, and I did that."

From the "the city of brotherly love," Jean moved to **Washington, D.C.** to initiate a writing and publishing project (*Record Vote Analysis*) for the Republican House Members of Congress. Later she joined Time-Life Books in nearby **Alexandria, Virginia**, first in edit research and then in publishing (marketing). She retired in 1986 and moved to northwest Arkansas in 1990.

~~

9. OUR ANIMALS

If the Name Fits

Anita French, Daily Record, March 1995

WHAT'S in a name? Not much, when it comes to cats. My cats were given names to reflect their personalities, but there was a slip-up somewhere. The two males, Chase and Sugar, could be named Stan and Ollie, for all it matters.

Chase was given his name because he liked to chase my oldest cat, Miss Kitty, when he was allowed to live in the house like decent people. He became an outside cat when I got tired of giving Miss Kitty CPR (that's cat purr resuscitation) every time Chase pursued her. She's an old gray cat who ain't what she used to be.

Sugar, on the other hand, got his name because he had such a sweet disposition I thought he was a female. So I made a mistake. So I never took a course in cat anatomy. Ex-cuse me.

You'd think that a male cat with a name like Chase wouldn't be afraid of anything. And if any creature from the forest primeval invaded his territory, you'd think Chase would be all over it like cat hairs on a black suit.

You'd think but you'd be wrong. There's a mangy marmalade cat that comes skulking around our house just to torment Chase and eat his food. For dessert, he once tore a piece out of Chase's ear. Chase is scared spitless of that cat.

I always know when old marmalade is around because I'll hear this sudden racket like someone falling over garbage cans, and then a loud scream. The scream belongs to Chase who, by the time I come out and chase his tormentor away, is either up a tree, on the roof or quaking under the eaves.

Sugar, on the other hand, isn't scared of anything that swishes its tail. The other night Marmalade came up to where Chase's food was and Sugar saw him through the screen door. Hearing a feral cry that chilled my blood, I crept up to see what was going on.

~ Comments ~

Chapter 9a

Anita: "Since this column was written, Chase and Sugar both ran away, or disappeared. I like to think that they're out there somewhere with Sugar protecting Chase from old Marmalade. As for Miss Kitty, at 80-plus something in cat years, she alone is still with me. Like her owner, she is a little older, a little heavier, a little grayer and a whole lot crankier. Miss Kitty endures—like her owner."

~~

Q. How does Miss Kitty get along with your husband's dog?
Anita: "They haven't met and never will."

~~

Cynthia: "We wonder why we ever added **involvement with animals** to our life commitments. Other people—the pacesetters—manage in cities and apartments. They lock their doors and leave to ski the Alps this season and dive the Greek Islands the next. They even rent their equipment; no commitments here. They are the ones who give us the ideas that we must always be first, always be thinking two steps ahead of the other guy, never resting, ceaselessly moving to the next thing."

~~

"Dogs have owners. Cats have staff"
—Anita's e-mail

There was Chase, cowering outside next to his food. There was Marmalade, crouching at the bottom of the steps ready to pounce. And there was Sugar—behind a screen door and holding the invader off by letting out an unearthly sound heard only in the deepest part of darkest Africa. It wasn't a growl; it was a primal scream.

Sugar practically went into a trance. He didn't move; he didn't waver. Marmalade was invading his space, and Sugar looked at him like he was cat litter. Even though there was a screen between them, Marmalade decided discretion was the better part of valor. He backed off and then disappeared into the night.

I was the sole observer of this fascinating little lesson in wildlife warfare, except for Miss Kitty. Being the grande dame that she is, she watched the whole episode as if she were Queen Elizabeth, and Sugar and Chase were Charles and Diana.

I told Sugar, "Way to go!" and then yelled out into the night, "Your mama, Marmalade!"

As for Chase he had disappeared, humiliated no doubt because he had been saved by a cute little number named Sugar. Chase is such a girly-cat. ★

A Curiosity to Their Mothers
Cynthia Haseloff, Morning News, October 2000

THIS column is about mules—equines that are a cross between a mare and a jack. Mules vary widely in size according to the size of the parents. Their color also varies. Appaloosa and Paint mules have become popular lately.

Generally mules are stronger than horses and smarter. They have good feet and, of course, big ears. A well cared for mule can be as slick and fat and handsome as any other equine. And they can do things horses can't—like jumping from a standing start, rising on their back feet like cats to clear fences.

A mule may be male or female, but it does not reproduce itself. Each mule is one of a kind, born a curiosity to its own mother—the horse half.

Mule contributions to building this country are undeniable. They pulled wagons going West, and plows that broke the prairies into fertile fields to feed a nation. They carried freight to the outlying settlements, hauled ore from the silver mines and bore supplies for the army.

General Crook, the Indian fighter, rode a mule exclusively in his pursuit of the last free tribes. Sometimes mule flesh fed both troopers and Indians.

Mule history is illustrious, but mules personally can't have high expectations. Their destiny, until recently when they became recreational animals, was hard work without much respect.

This sorry situation is undoubtedly processed early. Mules are smart. They don't waste time or energy like a horse does on flighty things. If they sense trouble, they are much more likely to wade in than run away. That's what makes them good pasture guardians.

Although some mules do become surly, ill tempered, stubborn and vengeful, a surprising number of the breed bear up, stepping up to the grim fare on their plates to do a remarkable thing. They rise above their circumstances and live lives of true dignity and worth.

These mules accept themselves and their role by excelling in their "muleness." They learn the routine and do their work without shirking.

My dad remembers how the mule teams of his father—a pair of bays and a pair of gray mules—pulled wagons in the fields where he and his brothers worked. Those mules

~ Comments ~

Chapter 9b

Cynthia: "A recent survey of people likely to vote revealed 75% believed the Democrat party symbol is a donkey—not a mule. Only 20% knew that both the donkey and the elephant were chosen as party symbols by a cartoonist—not by the parties to reflect their own ideals.

"In 1495 **Christopher Columbus** brought four jacks to America for producing mules. And the king of Spain, whose country so prized its jacks that it prohibited their exportation, later gave a wonderful animal to **George Washington**. Those royal jacks helped establish the American mule industry. The web site of **The International Horse Museum in Kentucky** is one of many Internet sources on equine activities."

~~

Pea Ridge, Arkansas is host to an annual **Mule Jump Contest** that originated late in the1980s. Mule owners from several states present an entertaining show held in the City Park on an October Saturday. At the 1990 contest the winning mule cleared a six-foot bar and set a world record that hasn't been beaten in 10 years of trying.

~~

anticipated the men, pulling the wagons without a driver to the next point of loading. My grandfather could talk to them, and they listened, seeming to understand, doing what he asked by voice not force.

Grandfather was not an easy man; he was not guilty of "the soft prejudice of low expectations." He believed a mule was capable and should learn to be worth its feed and purpose in life.

It was his job to make them useful and treat them well for the work they did. He thought mules were beautiful and kept them as slick and well groomed as his horses. Maybe he loved them better because they were workers.

It's hard not to respect the nobility of these half horses, and the brains and good sense of these half donkeys. By making the most of the lives they are given, they offer a lesson we humans can learn from mules. ★

~ Comments ~

Wasn't it Nietzsche who said, 'Writers are shameless about their adventures; they exploit them.' —Editor's note

10. BABIES IN ORGANIC TIME

Triplets at 55? No, Thanks!
Anita Creech, Morning News, February 2000

IT'S the story that many women my age still whisper about only to each other. No one else would understand. And they keep their voices low for fear the "fertility gods" might overhear.

In case you've forgotten (and we'd like to), a 55-year-old Washington woman and grandmother gave birth to triplets earlier this year. Thankfully, the three little girls were healthy, each one weighing in at about 3 to 5 pounds apiece. They were delivered by Cesarean section.

The mother already had eight children and is the grandmother of 13. At the time, medical experts said it was extremely rare for a woman in her fifties to bear triplets without the aid of fertility drugs.

Well, no kidding, Drs. Kildare. There's a reason for that. Most women in their fifties don't go around having babies voluntarily. And we would no more take fertility drugs than chew glass. That's because the idea of giving birth again is just about as appetizing.

Think about it. At an age when most of us are dealing with pre-menopausal repression, along comes post-partum depression to really send you over into the abyss.

Imagine the scenario. You're already suffering from sleep problems, and now you get to rise at 2 or 3 in the morning to feed the baby for several months. Well, what the heck. You're up anyway, right? If you're having a hot flash, you can splash some of that formula in your face.

Next comes potty training, when you're just beginning to deal with bladder difficulties of your own. Now you and your child can really "bond." Awaiting you down the road is the first day of school, homework, brown bag lunches, pimples, prom dresses and teenage angst. (Not theirs. Yours.)

Haven't we been there and done that—rather ineptly the first time? Isn't there some law written on stone tablets in a cave somewhere that women in their fifties shouldn't have to go through this again?

"Women over 50 don't have babies because they would put them down and forget where they left them."
— Anita's e-mail

Chapter 10a

Anita: "I received a lot of mail and comments about this column—all from women who knew exactly what I was talking about. Men don't have a clue."

~~

What would you have liked to be if you hadn't chosen to write?

Anita: "Switchboard operator."

Cynthia: "Doctor, architect or lawyer."

Jean: "I experienced several mid-life crises when I ventured to switch from journalism to some other occupation.

"In the late 1960s I spent two-and-one-half years learning about and selling life and health insurance. I sold myself adequate life and disability income insurance, learned techniques of selling and the basic value and purpose of life and health insurance for a self-sufficient lifestyle. A "too good to refuse" offer from **Farm Journal** changed that career plan.

"In the 1970s after leaving Farm Journal, I taught two beginning writing classes at **Temple University**, enrolled in two graduate courses (using computers in research and surveying freelance opportunities in Philadelphia). Then I took an extensive battery of tests at the university to determine what I should be when I grew up.

It's not that we don't love little babies or children. It's just that, while we may now have the wisdom we lacked as 20-year-old mothers, our stamina and energy have aged 30 years. The old gray mare just ain't what she needs to be.

Oh, I admit that once in awhile I see a baby and get all misty-eyed and think how nice it would be to have a little one in the house again. That's when I get a cat.

Other women fulfill this need with grandchildren. That's why they're called that. As in "These are somebody else's children. Isn't life grand?"

After the birth, the aforementioned grandmama/new mama was quoted as saying she felt fine and happy and that she was looking forward to having three newborns in the house again.

This sounds like whistling through the graveyard to me. ★

~Comments~

Chapter 10a continued

"The counselor's suggestion based on the results: "Go to law school at night for five years to obtain a degree and then specialize in arbitration law." Five years of night school starting at age 45?

"I opted to take a night course in Business Law at the Wharton Evening School of Business before moving on to government work in D.C.

"Later I worked for more than a year with two former IBM men who had formed a counseling firm. We conducted on-site surveys in Wilmington, Delaware and Washington. After analyzing the data, the men recommended word and data processing office equipment configured to help employees accomplish their tasks in a cost-effective manner. I **organized** several **seminars** for agency employees to introduce our services; subsequently, we conducted surveys for the Organization of American States **(OAS)** and the legal department of a **U.S. Treasury** office in DC.

"Finally I decided to stick with what I knew best; and signed on with **Time-Life Books**—after a 17-year hiatus from the company—to take advantage of considerable corporate benefits for retirement. I'm appreciative of the intervening experiences and gratified that I chose to shore up my retirement prospects when I did.

"Looking to the future **Bill Gates** said (in Chapter 11d) that 'people and companies will have to be open to reinventing themselves—possibly more than once'. I think he has that right."

~ ~

Organic Time Is Precious

Cynthia Haseloff, Morning News, July 2000

LIKE many adults I can't seem to recapture that sense of the endless day described by Harper Lee in her book *To Kill A Mockingbird*. "A day was twenty-four hours long but seemed longer," she wrote.

At this point in life, I'm time challenged, having no sense of the endless day, only of the endless tasks. I'm so grateful when I can fall into my chair for some mind-numbing television before nine o'clock at night.

This sense of too little time seems to be universal. A recent e-mail from an editor encouraged me to send some revisions on a book. The editor, a busy woman with a pre-teen, apologized for pressing: "Too much to do on this end and, darn it, it's summer! I want to play."

I wrote back, "It's summer here too."

It was a sad little exchange expressing our sense of loss for those summer days past when time was not organized with watches or anchored with tasks given high, low and no priority.

It was an organic thing, natural, bounded by sunrise, long twilight and peaceful slumber. Organic time is simply whatever time it takes—ever variable—generally free of trivial manmade clocks.

Have we forgotten that we ourselves are organic? We are not machines. We glance at a sunset we know we shouldn't miss. Great, we say, and rush off to the next task.

We need 'Not To Do' lists. At the top put: 'Don't try to be all things to all people.' Reserve some time for not doing anything and not feeling guilty about it.

A couple of weeks ago I was at an event—the third I had prepared for and attended that Friday and Saturday. I was tired of everything, pooped out with ought to, have to and should.

I surprised myself by saying suddenly, I've had enough. I'm going home. At home I went out and worked with my critters—truly enjoyed cleaning their pens, taking the time needed instead of rushing through it to another task. Fellowshipping with other passengers on this earth who do not talk can be rewarding.

~ Comments ~

"We are greedy winners of some time lottery. With an abundance of available time, we become profligate. We are time-aholics, unable to quit filling time. We keep adding things to our days, fearful that we will be without something to do and have to face our nakedness. At last we discover that we have time for tasks we hate and people we don't enjoy, but none for the things and the ones we love."
—Cynthia Haseloff

Chapter 10b

Cynthia: "We lost natural time with the invention of the electric light bulb—or perhaps even with the firelight in the cave that let people rise above organic time, that made them believe they had 'extra' time. Over the centuries came all the labor saving devices and everything else that tells us it saves us time. I personally don't have time for another labor/time saving device.

"A documentary I once saw on the transportation of the Jews of Europe to concentration camps showed a conscientious young man running to catch the train to Auschwitz. Some days I wonder if I'm running to catch the train to Auschwitz.

"With so much time filled, we've become patchers on the unrolling fabric of time—a quick patch here and a quick patch there. We slap a quick fix on this relationship, grow irritable when a child can't get socks on to meet our deadline.

"We forget that children need time to dawdle. Their little brains require some time to do nothing but form pathways, and so do ours.

I suspect horse people, animal and plant people have a compelling need for organic time that others may not have. Perhaps some of us actually, genetically need to be in contact in our highly civilized world with time not found on clocks. A lifestyle built around horses and animals may provide a means to that ancient system.

Organic time cannot be compressed. It takes nine months for a human baby, eleven for a colt. Organic time is the time required for a seed to put out roots and leaves, the time to make a kitten, puppy or horse tame and trusting, a member of the household, a companion in work and play. Organic time is the time to live one life, to love and work and grow old.

This organic time is the tide we swim in—inevitable, not to be rushed. The elixir restores and renews us. Like amphibians, we must return to it from time to time in order to survive. ★

~ Comments ~

Chapter 10b continued

"We should quit defining ourselves by what we do rather than who we are, and forget being generous with all of our time. Reserve some for not doing anything and not feeling guilty about it."
~~
"You don't stop laughing because you grow old. You grow old because you stop laughing."
—Anita's e-mail.
~~

11. ESCAPE

A Day at the Flea Markets

Anita Creech, Morning News, February 2000

E VERY now and then, a friend and I make it a point
to visit Pineville, Missouri, a small town just across the
state line that lies along the Elk River. What we love about
the place is its quaint square, circa 1800s courthouse and an
old-fashioned grocery store across the street.

The store is about as old as the courthouse. It's the only
one where we have found Amish-made noodles, and a
garrulous butcher who makes his own chili and a daily lunch
special for customers.

We also drop in at The Pineville Grill. It's not just a visit
to the past; it is the past. This diner has no pretensions.
Customers sit in vinyl-covered booths or on metal chairs,
resting their feet on a carpet worn thin by years of use.
Overhead, ceiling fans whir next to an exposed air duct that
runs the length of the room

But patrons don't come to The Pineville Grill for
atmosphere—they come for the food. Nothing fancy, mind
you, just good old-fashioned burgers, chicken in a basket or
dinners with all the fixings.

And don't forget the dessert. Next to its famous Pineville
burger, the Grill is most noted for its homemade pies turned
out by owner Linda Rivard.

No visit to Pineville would be complete without taking
in the flea markets. These are such fascinating places. Where
else can a person find such things as an Elvis lamp? Or, for
the serious collector, a bunch of marked-down Beanie Babies?

I love flea markets because they are a stroll through history
and a refresher course in Americana.

Who can visit one and not find something from their
childhood or that their family used? Old electric fans with
big metal blades that made an awful racket. Toasters with
pull-down sides. Telephones with rotary dials. Portable record
players that came in a case. And 45-rpm vinyl records. Try
finding those anywhere in today's music stores. Heck, just
try finding a record player. They've also become history, which

~ Comments ~

> "I love flea markets because they are a
> stroll through history and a refresher
> course in Americana."
> —Anita Creech

Chapter 11a

**Q. Anita, what are your favorite
Arkansas getaways?**
"**Eureka Springs** because, despite its
touristy aspect and some of the
tackiness that goes along with that, it is
a most charming city and wonderful
weekend getaway. A friend and I love to
escape here for a good lunch at one of
the city's wonderful eateries and then
just walk around to enjoy the
atmosphere.

"Another favorite is **Altus** (off I-40)
where several vineyards and a wine
festival in the fall make for lots of
singing and dancing and general gaiety.

"I also recommend the **Fayetteville
Square** on a Sunday. It is serene and
lovely to look at."

And during the Christmas season,
Fayetteville and Bentonville **downtown
squares** are ablaze with white lights.
~~
Jean: "**Flea markets** abound in NW
Arkansas and neighboring states. After
moving to Bella Vista from Washington,
DC in 1990, I rented a flea market
booth in Bella Vista and sold furniture
and furnishings not needed in my new
home. It was such fun I continued
'feeding it' for two and one-half years.
Keeping the booth stocked meant
attending lots of garage and estate
sales and after two years I tired of that.
It seemed time to return to my writing
and publishing."

~~

is why flea markets have boxes and boxes of long-playing records that sell for a buck or 50 cents apiece.

But one of the best things about flea markets is some of the people we meet there. The last time my friend and I visited the one in Pineville, an older woman struck up a conversation while waiting at the cash register. She regaled the cashier and us with a story about her once being betrothed to a man who, instead of buying her an engagement ring, gave her a set of pots and pans. Insulted, she called off the wedding. The spurned suitor later became a preacher, she said.

Men can be such practical things. My husband once brought me a can of peaches as a gift. Another time it was a box of crackers, a package of spaghetti and a jar of mayonnaise. It was better than getting a set of Corning Ware, I guess.

All this has me thinking. If everyday things that fall out of use are destined to become collector's items, I've got a house full of stuff that will make me rich some day.

Yeah, right, and Florida ballots don't have dimples. ★

~ Comments ~

Chapter 11a continued

The Morning News (30 September 2001) reported that for 210 years the population center has consistently moved south and west from Chestertown, Maryland (1790 census).

"**The center of population** is creeping slowly toward **Northwest Arkansas**. If the current trend continues, the center could reach here by 2040.

"The center has taken 40 years to travel the last 180 miles—from Centralia, Illinois (1960) to Edgar Springs" (2000), according to Fred Broome, **US Geodetic Survey**. "If the rate slows, the US population center might not reach our area until near the turn of the next century" (3000). It is not a matter of density; but means half of the population lives north of the point, half south. And the east-west population is also evenly divided.
—Dan Craft, reporter.

~~

City Life "ain't restful"
Anita French, Daily Record, September 1994

THERE is a way of life beyond city borders that spins itself out day after day, unnoticed and unheralded. Here there are no housing tracts being built, no ugly electrical poles going up, no new businesses moving in.

Drive up the highway towards Powell, Missouri. Flea markets, farms and mobile homes with rusty cars as yard ornaments share the landscape. Pretty soon you enter Albert E. Brumley country, where the well-known gospel music writer lived, and where each year hundreds of fans gather for a weekend songfest.

A little later down the road you'll come into Longview, aptly named because the surrounding area is flat and open. It looks like Kansas, and trucks hauling large bales of hay drive through the main intersection. If you're hungry, stop at the Longview Restaurant—and step into the past.

The friendly waitress, wearing T-shirt and shorts, waves you to a table covered by a plastic tablecloth. On top are mismatched salt and pepper shakers and a metal napkin holder. On the wall hangs a plastic wreath decorated with colorful Easter eggs. The waitress comes to your table and asks what you'd like to drink.

Water? "It's sulfur, honey," she warns, so you order a Coke instead, which is brought to you in a can along with a plastic glass filled with ice. The Coke is teeth-hurting cold and tastes good.

There's a buffet offering salad, fried chicken, mashed potatoes and gravy, green beans, corn, fried fish, turkey with dressing and Jell-o. There's also fruit cocktail and homemade blueberry cobbler. Everything tastes just fine, thank you very much, and the coffee is great.

The after-church crowd has thinned out and just a few couples and locals remain. Most of the men wear billed caps advertising something agricultural, and the women have on neat cotton dresses.

Everyone smiles at you but no one tries to invade your privacy. A few customers gang up at the cash register and the waitress calls out, "Daddy, will you ring up those people?" On your way out you pick up a toothpick at the counter.

~ Comments ~

Chapter 11b

'Ain't' is included in the dictionary, but is not a word Anita uses often. In this instance she is quoting **Satchel Paige** so the word that makes some strict grammarians cringe is appropriate here.

~~

Decorating Styles
Jean: "In the 1970s a young law student, who worked as one of the writers on a publishing project for the Republican members of congress, got me interested in astrology. He was a real zodiac fan and persuaded me to buy a paperback book he had recommended. Interesting for its entertainment value at least. Zodiac signs are the best key to our own personal style, according to astrologer and author Greg Polkosnik.

The three column writers in this book were born under the signs of Cancer (June 22-July 23) or Leo (July 24-August 23). Here is Polkosnik's interpretation of "our decorating styles."

Jean (**Cancer**) The "least likely to go over the top." Born under the most conservative sign regarding decorating, Cancer children are also the most secure.

Leos Anita and Cynthia are labeled with the key phrase "pure, unbridled creativity." The Leo's design is not about modesty. What's hanging on the walls is more important than the color of the walls. They use color liberally without reservation, Polkosnik opined.

For the interest of you who were born under different signs, here follows a brief description from an aesthetic perspective. We leave it to close friends to decide on the accuracy of these attributes.

~~

If you need to fill your gas tank before leaving, there's a store just across the street that also offers ice, cold drinks, food, maps, auto repair and a bank. Your basic one-stop.

Continuing on your journey, the landscape suddenly pulls a trick before your eyes, and the flat lands turn abruptly into a lush forest, named after that somewhat famous Missouri boy, Mark Twain. On the way home, you wander through Roaring River State Park, Washburn, Lost Bridge, Garfield, Gateway and Pea Ridge.

It's when you reach the site of the famous Civil War battle in Pea Ridge that you look out over those "vasty fields" and remember what was lost here. And you wonder if that's what America is best at—losing things.

It would be nice to think that the land and life that lie outside of our daily bustle will be preserved. We need it as a place to go and replenish the spirit.

City life offers much, but the same thing can be said about it that Satchel Paige once commented about the "social ramble."

"Avoid it," he said. "It ain't restful." ★

~Comments~

Chapter 11b continued

Aries – Most masculine, nothing prissy. Avant-garde without gimmicks.
Taurus – The most tactile. How one feels in a room of furniture is more important than the look of the pieces.
Gemini – Like teenagers, flighty, tough to pin down and thriving on change.
Virgo – Style is "a place for everything and everything in its place."
Libra – Uptown sophistication, opulent without excess.
Scorpio – Keyed in to the primal side of nature with birth, death, sex and religion in their decorating schemes.
Sagittarius – Style of multiculturalism with nothing taboo; tend to be idealists.
Capricorn – Known for material nature, they would rather sit on wooden crates than settle for buying anything they perceive as cheap.
Aquarius – True eccentrics of the zodiac; seek unique pieces, love technology and gadgets.
Pisces – Their style is about mixing rather than matching. Up close, a room may look a mess, but step back and you see a work of art.
—*Arkansas Democrat Gazette*, December 2001.

~~

Every Child Is Gifted

Cynthia Haseloff, Morning News, August 2000

AS a young snob I thought kids who did not go to school were losers. Until I saw it happen, I did not realize that learning could take place outside of school.

Many boys about fourteen or fifteen showed up to work for my dad. Most were dropouts or kicked outs, having no purpose, and motorcycle payments to make. Some were considered hyperactive or learning disabled, and had been put in special classes that labeled them that way.

My dad would soon have these boys doing men's work. He taught them to think about what they were doing and how to do it best. "Where was your head?" he often asked. There were giggles many times because the boys knew where he meant. He was hard. The work was hard and useful, not busy work.

My dad and mother—Tommie and Virginia Haseloff—never met a child that didn't have a unique identity and that could not learn. They worked with whatever the child had. Low expectations never helped anyone.

My father did not work with identifiable groups. He considered each of the boys as people and rewarded them with time to rest, talk and drink a Coke. Every one of the kids learned to hit golf balls well.

When he said they'd done something well, they knew they had. They had earned his praise. And in their minds they'd accomplished something worth doing. They'd learned something important in the world they wanted to learn in.

One of the boys was considered slow by the school system and had been put into special classes. He could not talk in a way that anyone could really understand. His words sounded more like grunts and groans than speech.

My mother worked on that. She'd have him "slow down" and repeat words until they came out clearly and she could understand. By the end of the summer, anyone could understand him. He had a lot to say.

He could also do math. He learned it from my mother as she had him figure his wages and deductions for withholding taxes.

~ Comments ~

> _"Recently I was introduced as the mother of Senator Fulbright of Arkansas. At once I detected they had never heard of Senator Fulbright, never heard of Arkansas, and definitely never desired to hear of me. The populace still needs education, I tell you."_
> —Roberta Fulbright, 1945

Chapter 11c

Cynthia: "In recent months, I've met a lot of kids who are achievers and leaders on horseback. I've seen four- and six-year-olds on horseback making horses do what the horses are supposed to do.

"As adults touching the lives of young people we have an opportunity to make the world better by seeing each child as unique and a gift to the future, by helping each child become her or his best self.

"I've seen a young man repeatedly throw a rope over a log, patiently teaching younger children his roping art. I've seen that same young fellow study a locked trailer door for which the keys had been lost. He found a solution.

"While the adult owner arranged for a bolt cutter, the boy simply unscrewed two hinge bolts and opened the door.

"Youngsters like Cody may not participate in the popular school sports or the student council. Many teachers will think them odd in their boots, jeans and big belt buckles. These teachers will never know what leadership potential they are missing. They will never see what fine human beings they are, never know that these children are the heart and foundation of the country."

~~

In recent months, I've met a lot of kids who are achievers and leaders on horseback. I've seen four- and six-year-olds making their horses do what horses were supposed to do.

I've seen a young man repeatedly throw a rope over a log, patiently teaching younger children his roping art. I've seen that same young fellow study a locked trailer door for which the keys had been lost. He found a solution.

While the adult owner arranged for a bolt cutter, he simply unscrewed two bolts and opened the door. Youngsters like Cody may not participate in the popular school sports or the student council. Many teachers will think them odd in their boots, jeans and big belt buckles.

These teachers will never know what leadership potential they are missing. They will never see what fine human beings they are, never know that these children are the heart and foundation of the country.

Every August is time for a new choice. Will it be back to school, back to failure? Or back to school, back to the promise of every child's potential? ★

~ Comments ~

Chapter 11c continued

Teamwork is the ability to work together toward a common vision. The ability to direct individual accomplishment toward organizational objectives. It is the fuel that allows common people to attain uncommon results.
—Cynthia's e-mail

Reading Is A Great Escape

FOR ROSE CHRISTENSEN'S *READING COACH*
Jean Strong, Daily Record, July 1997

TODAY'S frontiers are as fascinating as those of the distant past. I am reminded of this as I pursue simultaneous reading of several books distributed around my house.

In his 1988 book titled *1999: Victory without War*, Richard M. Nixon outlined what we must do in the closing years of the 20th century to ensure peace in the 21st. "The choice before mankind will be not just whether we make the future better than the past, but whether we will survive to enjoy the future." Heavy but interesting.

While Nixon talks hopefully of peace, Bill Gates, in *The Road Ahead*, fixes his attention on the Information Highway—another challenge and frontier to the future. He suggests ways the personal computer (PC) can make our lives better—like programming your telephone to not ring during dinner if the call is for you.

Gates' view is that "the information highway won't be a sudden, revolutionary creation but that the Internet, along with evolution in the PC and PC software, will guide us step by step to the full system . . . People and companies will have to be open to reinventing themselves—possibly more than once," he tells us.

The Clare Booth Luce biography, *Rage for Fame* by Sylvia Jukes Morris, provides a titillating look at New York cafe society in the early 1900s, and how Clare repeatedly reinvented herself in her climb to the top.

I saw Ambassador Luce in the late 1950s speaking at Fourth of July festivities in Boston. Her husband, Henry Luce, proprietor of the magazine empire where I was employed, sat beside the podium; his gaze was firmly fixed on Clare in the reverse manner of Pat watching Dick perform.

I remember she misspoke: "As your ambassador to Russia . . . er-r-r . . . Italy…." No doubt she would have preferred Russia for her ambassadorial duty. More power.

Watching and reading about Mrs. Luce and her impressive career as playwright, journalist, U.S. congresswoman and ambassador was continually fascinating.

~ Comments ~

> Never argue with a woman who knows how to read. It's likely she can also think.
> —Anita's e-mail

Chapter 11d

Q. Anita, what books do you enjoy?
"I'm a big fan of English mysteries, especially those by **P.D. James** and **Edmund Crispin**. I also like **Sue Grafton** and **Tony Hillerman**. But one of the best books I've read in recent years was nonfiction and called *Rising Tide: The Great Mississippi Flood of 1927 and How It Changed America*," **James M. Barry**. He describes how the flood changed politics and life in the flooded cities. The book reads like a novel and I couldn't put it down."

~~

> "Without books, history is silent, science crippled, thought and speculation at a standstill."
> —Barbara Tuchman

Ellen Williamson's paperback *When We Went First Class* is a recollection of good times during the same period. As Clare climbed from poverty to riches, Ellen Williamson moved in affluent circles among social sets in Cedar Rapids (Iowa) San Francisco, New York, Europe and Asia. She makes a delightfully humorous tale of it, too.

Henry Grunwald's autobiography, *One Man's America*, offers thoughtful, humane commentary. A print journalist at Time Incorporated, he later became ambassador to his native Austria.

The late Jane Howard, a LIFE colleague in the 1950s, chronicled the lives of women on the frontier of the women's movement in the 1960s. As one who never marched in a demonstration, I am enjoying Jane's account of it all in *A Different Woman*. Delightful and insightful.

My own book published last fall focuses on yesterday's frontier—an eyewitness account when all territory west of the Mississippi was considered the Wild West. Title: *A Prairie Almanac: 1839 to 1919, the eyewitness story of everyday life of pioneers as told by Isaac N. Kramer.* ★

~ Comments ~

<u>Chapter 11d continued</u>

Arguing with Woman Is Risky

A couple was vacationing at a fishing resort up north. The husband liked to fish at dawn. The wife liked to read. One morning the husband returned after several hours of fishing and decided to take a short nap. Although she wasn't familiar with the lake, the wife decided to take the boat. She rowed out a short distance, anchored, and returned to reading her book.

Along came the sheriff in his boat. He pulled up alongside. "Good morning, Ma'am. What are you doing?"

"Reading my book," she replied, thinking to herself, "Isn't it obvious?"

"You're in a restricted fishing area," he informed her.

"But officer, I'm not fishing. Can't you see that?"

"Yes, but you have all the equipment. I'll have to take you in and write you up."

"If you do that, I'll have to charge you with rape," snapped the irate woman.

"But, I haven't even touched you," groused the sheriff.

"Yes, that's true," she replied, "but you do have all the equipment."

—Jean's e-mail

12. HELPFUL CRITICISM

No More Biblical Movies, Please

Anita Creech, Morning News, September 2000

OH NO! The television networks are planning to show more movies based on the Bible this fall. Someone tell them 'Thou shalt not.' These movies are about as truthful as pop-Christianity. Just as my teeth grind when I see the name of God or Jesus Christ reduced to a bumper sticker slogan, I always squirm in embarrassment over movies like Cecil B. DeMille's "The Ten Commandments."

Who can ever forget this film's immortal line uttered by Anne Baxter as Nefretiri: "Oh Moses, Moses. You sweet, stubborn, adorable fool," or some such idiocy.

Equally unforgettable was Edward G. Robinson playing the villain Dathan. Most famous for his gangster roles, Robinson didn't fit anyone's image of a biblical character. Any minute I expected him to snarl, "I'm gonna get Moses, see." In fact, I kept waiting for him to use his closing line from the classic gangster film "Little Caesar."

"Mother of mercy!" he asked, "Is this the end of Dathan?" One could only hope so.

I enjoyed DeMille's movie when I was younger, but I have put away childish things. Now when I hear Baxter say, "Oh Moses, Moses," all I can do is groan "Oh, brother," and quickly turn the channel. The special effects are great—at least they were for their time. But Hollywood never has and never will produce a movie about the Bible that is truthful. Too boring, they say. Got to spice it up and add dialogue that isn't there.

So, who asked them? Makes you wish a few locusts or leaping frogs were sent down to plague these misguided filmmakers.

You can also count among Hollywood's biblical disasters the 1950s "King of Kings" starring Jeffrey Hunter as a blue-eyed, blond-haired Jesus, and George Stevens' unintentionally ironic "The Greatest Story Ever Told."

~ Comments ~

"They were sincere words and put together honestly."
—W. J. Lemke, University of Arkansas journalism department, after reading through the nearly two million words of Roberta's daily columns "As We See It."

Chapter 12a

Anita does have favorite movies, and memorable lines that tickled her. Take **"Casablanca,"** the classic 1942 (the year she was born) film, and her all-time favorite movie. She can recite the dialog.

"Humphrey Bogart, proprietor of 'Rick's,' is being questioned by police Captain Renault, played by Claude Rains. When he asks Rick why he came to Casablanca, Bogart replies that he came for the waters.

"Waters. What waters? We're in the desert," says Rains.
"I was misinformed," Bogart deadpans.

The film's theme song, **"As Time Goes By,"** is Anita's favorite love song. The last 2001 issue of MM magazine lists the song as No. 4 favorite among its readers. Only "Stardust," "God Bless America" and "White Christmas" were more popular. "Over the Rainbow"—named top song of the 20th century by the National Endowment of the Arts and the Recording Industry of America—ranked fifth with MM readers.

~~

Don Hewitt, CBS' veteran producer of *60 Minutes*, has written a memorable book titled **Tell Me a Story, Fifty Years and 60 MINUTES in Television** (Public Affairs, 2001). This fast and enjoyable read provides insight into corporate America's impact on news reporting.

Hewitt writes: "If there was a working model for *60 Minutes*, it was *Life* magazine, the old *Life* that came out weekly and was regarded as a family friend in the homes of millions of Americans. It made the kind of

And we won't even talk about the ridiculous "Last Temptation of Christ." At the time, I hoped it was the last movie by director Martin Scorsese.

These filmmakers mean well, you say? Well, no, they don't. They mean to make money, whether it's off the Bible or anything else they can lay their greedy little hands on. I wish they'd just stick to their usual grimy fare, and go and sin no more. ★

~ Comments ~

Chapter 12a continued

connection with the audience I wanted, and I wasn't above stealing the idea lock, stock and barrel. . .. While **journalism is the principal business of great newspapers**, it is not the principal business of great television networks. It is a very small part of the corporate culture and thus a very small part of its concerns," Hewitt wrote.

~~

Jean: "Although I don't claim to know **Don Hewitt**, he extended a professional courtesy when we both were covering the crash of an airplane with an altimeter problem one February night in the late 1950s. I worked for *Life* and Hewitt for CBS News. We wanted to photograph recovery of bodies from the East River, preferably strapped in their seats, as my editor put it. This was among the early big airliner crashes.

"I had hired a motor boat for the *Life* team's vigil. For his camera crew, Hewitt leased the tugboat that had rescued a few crash survivors that first night. On the evening of the third day on the East River, Hewitt kindly invited me aboard to interview the tug's captain. In the pitch-dark wheelhouse I made brief notes in my spiral notebook. The captain described the horror of being unable to respond to the cries for help because a sandbar prevented his getting the tug close to the sinking plane.

"Later, at the hospital, I interviewed a survivor who swam to the tug after extricating himself and a young boy from the sinking wreckage. As I left his hospital room, he cautioned, "Don't make me out a hero. I ain't no hero." He had been unable to release fellow passengers who were trapped in their seats in the tail section.

"Neither interview was used. At *Life*, the picture magazine, if you didn't get a unique picture, you didn't have a usable story. Competition for space was fierce between the Foreign and Domestic news departments.

Back to School, Back to Failure?

Cynthia Haseloff, Morning News, August 2000

FOR many children, back to school is back to failure. They will not find the road to success, only another affirmation of their inadequacy and unimportance. Once I would have fought over a statement like that, but now I know it is true.

Every institution has a natural constituency—a target group that they serve well. The kids who are best-served in schools are those who prosper in the system, within the structure of education. They are bright-eyed, eager hand wavers who know the answers, and expect to be rewarded for it.

An educator once called them the concrete sequential learners. They catch on quickly to the system, to what is explained in class or read in books and move from step to step without looking to the side. They are the ideal student for teachers who themselves were probably concrete sequential learners.

These kids are the backbone of the education system, its mainstay. They are the academic achievers. We are proud of them as they win scholarships and finish college and graduate school. Other students are not well served. If education were a business they would be dissatisfied customers. A conscientious company would direct them elsewhere or they would find another source for their need to learn.

Meanwhile two-thirds of students who are not academic achievers lose out, just as their parents and grandparents did.

So what's the problem? Educators are bright people looking for answers to a crumbling education system. It's not so hard, I think. Kids need to be told and to know that they count as people and that what they are doing amounts to something.

Some kids come into the education system so scarred by their family life and poverty that they may never find the self-confidence and faith required for learning. As a society we will have to recognize this and work very hard to overcome the attitudes and mind sets that destroy lives.

Good kids from good homes who just don't "get school" sometimes end up quitting or are kicked out. Keeping them

~ Comments ~

> *"About the only fun I get these days is turning the other cheek."*
> —Roberta Fulbright, 1945, when her editorial campaigns evoked vocal opposition.

Chapter 12b

Cynthia: "Every August is time for a new choice. Will it be back to school, back to failure?

"As a teacher, I had **too many students that I did not get to know**. We shuffle kids all day from teacher to teacher, room to room. No teacher with a full room gets to know the quietly frustrated kids, their needs and potential. We know the smart ones and the disruptive ones. They take our time. But we miss so much."

~~

Man without Medicine by Cynthia Haseloff is a good **read-aloud book**. It takes the reader and listener(s) on an adventure in the company of a Kiowa Indian and a throwaway Indian boy. They get acquainted while pursuing horse thieves across the prairie, and the boy learns about his heritage. It is a delight and thought provoking.
—Jean Strong

~~

Jean: "Newspapers and television share problems resulting from **corporate ownership**. Magazines do, too. In the 1950s, founder Henry Luce was still the benevolent proprietor of **Time, Inc.** which harbored a small fleet of magazines including *Life*, the picture weekly.

"Television came along to provide instant photo coverage of colorful and newsworthy events and usurped an increasing share of advertising dollars. The weekly *Life* finally ceased publication in the late 1970s and was resurrected as a monthly before it died a second time. Time, Inc. eventually became Time-Warner and is now **AOL**

in school becomes cruel and unusual punishment for them, their teachers and their parents.

What's wrong with these young people? Can't they see the opportunities they are missing? Can't they see the dismal future ahead without a formal education? Maybe they can't see. They really are young and ignorant of the possibilities of life. But they also really know what is not working for them.

Might the answer be "honor the child, respect the committed teacher"? Give teachers the help needed to know their students, and insist that they do make the effort to know them. But don't leave it all to the teacher or the school. As a teacher, I had too many students that I did not get to know.

We shuffle kids all day from teacher to teacher, room to room. No teacher with a full room gets to know the quietly frustrated kids, their needs and potential. We know the smart ones and the disruptive ones. They take our time. But we miss so much.

If there is a single thing that would help education, it is reducing class size so those teachers can know their students and work more often one on one. Miracles can happen when children and teachers work together for the individual student's growth. ★

~Comments ~

Chapter 12b continued

Time Warner—a big corporate umbrella for a conglomerate of Internet, entertainment and media enterprises. "The 'tell me a story' approach of the old *Life* and Hewitt's 60 MINUTES might also accurately describe a columnist's task?"

~~

"As the ownership of American news media becomes more and more concentrated, with all outlets subject to judgment by some 25-year-old hotshot on Wall Street as to whether they 'meet earnings expectations,' the pressure to cut news gathering gets worse. As far as the media conglomerates are concerned, newspapers and television networks are just 'profit centers'."
—Molly Ivins, November 2001

13. THE HEALTH BUSINESS

Visiting the Doctor
Anita French, Daily Record, October 1993

NEXT to having my upper lip caught in a vise, visiting the doctor is my second favorite thing to do. Where else can you go and waste an hour in the waiting room reading a 1979 issue of *Fertility* magazine?

You also run into the most interesting people such as the patient who has been there so many times she knows every doctor by his first name, takes her own blood pressure and has a wing named for her.

I was in a waiting room once where a big lumbering farmer wearing overalls and an eye patch kept staring at everybody with his good eye. I entertained myself by wondering how he got hurt. Hit in the eye with a cow patty, maybe?

Inevitably, there is the child with the cold who insists on being your bosom buddy. After wiping his runny nose with his hand and then offering you a gumball with same, he seals the friendship by sneezing all over your magazine. That's when I'd like to lean over and whisper, "Hey, kid. You're going to get a shot with a big needle."

If you're a first-time patient, you have to fill out those forms that tell them where to send the bill. Of course they try to disguise this by asking you all sorts of medical questions. On one I filled out recently, some of the questions were: "Do you drink? Smoke? Chew? Dip?" I was sorely tempted to say yes to all of them, just to see if they were paying attention.

And there are so many other fun things to do at the doctor's office. After cooling your heels in the waiting room for 30 minutes, the nurse escorts you to another room and then says, "The doctor will be right with you," a statement that should rank up there with the other don't-you-believe-it classics, such as "The check is in the mail."

To make your wait more comfortable, the nurse hands you what looks like a giant napkin with armholes, tells you to put it on and climb up on something that resembles a medieval torture device. So you sit, wearing a paper blouse with no buttons or bows, your legs dangling, and trying to

~ Comments ~

> "What can you expect of a profession that tells its patients to wee inside a paper cup and then carry it around for everyone to see?"
> —Anita French, 1993

Chapter 13a

Three hospitals in northwest Arkansas will soon line I-540 in Bentonville, Rogers and Fayetteville.

Fayetteville's Washington Regional Medical Center (181 beds) is the first to move west to the Interstate (summer 2002). The **Bentonville** groundbreaking for its Northwest Medical Center of Benton County hospital (128 beds) took place in 2001 and will replace the Bates Medical Center. St. Mary's hospital in **Rogers** is exploring ways to move its facility between Bentonville and Fayetteville along I-540. Scheduled: 220 beds for completion in 2005.

This is good news for the growing population and is attracting more health personnel and advanced health technology to serve the people.

~~

"You don't stop laughing because you grow old. You grow old because you stop laughing."
—Anita's e-mail

ignore those metal stirrups that are jutting out on the sides like gargoyles.

To pass the time, you begin to cast your wary eyes around the room. But unless you're into things like tongue depressors and cotton balls, there's not much to look at. Just about the time you start counting the holes in the ceiling's acoustic tiles, the doctor finally walks in.

Now, most doctors I've been to were friendly, gentle and thorough. But every once in awhile I've run across one who thinks he's making bread and you're the dough.

When he starts kneading some parts as if he were picking out casabas, that's when I would love to grab his stethoscope and scream into it "SOCIALIZED MEDICINE!"

But then, doctors can be such fey creatures. The one who delivered my son sat out in the hall while I was in labor and cracked jokes with the nurses. Every time they'd laugh, he would glance toward me to see if I thought it was funny, too. It was kind of hard to join the fun, however, when, as one woman described it, someone was trying to pull my upper lip over my head.

When they're not trying to be Henny Youngman, doctors like to invent all sorts of medical tests to give their patients another laugh. I don't know of anyone who hasn't had a good hee-haw while getting a barium test or a Pap smear.

But then what can you expect of a profession that tells its patients to wee inside a paper cup and then carry it around for everyone to see? I swear one of these days I'm going to fill that cup with apple juice and then drink it in front of the nurse so I can have a good laugh. ★

Men Patients Have Little Patience

Anita Creech, Morning News, June 2000

OLDER men share two unfailing traits. One, they don't need "no stinkin' map." Two, being a hospital patient is only for those who haven't been in combat.

I found out about trait No. 1 while growing up with my Dad. Trait No. 2 was revealed when my husband, an ex-Marine, went into the hospital recently.

Let me say right here that most women know the rules about hospitals. It starts when we give birth and lose such cherished virtues as modesty and privacy. When I was in labor, everybody in the hospital got to massage my parts like they were picking out melons.

Next came childhood where I received a crash course in stitches, broken limbs and midnight trips to the emergency room. The one thing I learned from all this is that you don't give a hard time to people who carry needles, give you oxygen or sign discharge papers. My husband apparently never heard of this life-enhancing rule.

His first few hours in the emergency room were OK because he was groggy and hooked up to machines. He became alert and restive, however, when moved to the intensive care unit. He apparently thought ICU meant "instant check up," for he wanted to know when he could leave.

The doctor said not for a few days, causing a look on my husband's face I knew was bad news.

The next morning, he wanted to go home for a few hours to check the mail and feed the dog—apparently thinking that a hospital is like a motel where he could leave and then pick up his key at the front desk when he returned. "Maybe they could stamp his hand," joked a friend.

Then he turned on me for not helping him escape. How come he only had a flimsy hospital gown to wear? Why didn't I bring him some street clothes, he asked suspiciously. Was I in cahoots with these people?

~Comments~

Chapter 13b

In December 1993, Anita penned a column for the *Daily Record* commenting on a TV anchorwoman's report about one company's solution to the age-old problem of men not putting down the toilet lid. Anita agreed with the CNN lady who said that a new beeping lid 'won't work.'

Anita: "Personally, I think it's unnatural for men and women to share a bathroom. . . . Men and women **sharing bathrooms** is contrary to the natural order of things. His and Her towels are not nearly enough. We need houses that have His and Her bathrooms."

~~

Jean: "We are fortunate in having so many small but interesting—even picturesque—towns in Arkansas, Missouri and Oklahoma—all within a day's drive. Wandering about is good for the soul and fun, too."

Yeah, honey, I wanted you to stay in the hospital so I could have the remote control to myself, sell our gold mine and run off with the red-headed kid who delivers pizza.

By that night my husband was in revolt. He got fed up with the IV that went where he went, so it went—out of his arm and on to the floor. He also pitched a small monitor that was taped to his chest. "He threw it in the trash can," a nurse told me solemnly the next morning.

I tried to act shocked, but all I could think was, "Way to go!"

So maybe it was no surprise that this was the day the doctor decided my husband could go home. When I told him, he began packing his bag with everything in the room, including the toilet paper and the discarded tubing from his IV. He had paid for it and so it was his, by gum.

When they brought around the wheelchair, my husband made his last stand. He thought it absurd that he would be steady on his feet only when he hit the outside sidewalk where the hospital's liability apparently ends.

Ours doesn't, however, as the bill is yet to arrive. When it does, I'm sure my outraged husband will return to the hospital to pick up whatever medical equipment he feels entitled to—like a dialysis machine. ★

Shall We Dance?

Anita Creech, Morning News, May 2000

I ALWAYS feel guilty on hearing that seniors need to exercise. My idea of exercise is making my king-sized bed each morning. And I can't do that without a coffee break. It doesn't help to work in a retirement community where most of the seniors are fit, tanned and active. Disgusting. Why can't they act their age?

"The average American lives a long time, but he or she is sedentary, fat (and) unfit," stated a recent article. "The worst impact is on older adults who have accumulated a lifetime of this comfortable but ultimately disabling lifestyle."

Go. Away. What's it to anybody if I enjoy a comfortable but disabling lifestyle of sitting in front of a computer all day and then staring at television all night.

My spirits perked up, however, when the article recommended that seniors start with ordinary walking or other exercise that is "not hard work." Does walking casually to the refrigerator count? How about strolling over to the king-sized bed and flopping down on it? Works for me.

Seniors have the same complaints about exercise as do their younger counterparts: It's boring. It hurts. They're too busy. Their horoscope warned them against it. They inherited a flawed gene from an ancestor who dropped dead while exercising on the deck of the *Mayflower.*

I don't like exercise because it's boring, it hurts and I'm too busy watching television. Still, I found a fun way to get some. Go dancing.

Once a week, my husband and I do a Fred and Ginger routine at a dance held at a senior citizens center. The band plays country music so I guess it's more of a Freddy Bob and Ginger Sue routine. We do a little two-stepping, a little waltzing, a little line dancing—all to a little night music.

Most of the couples who come stay until the dance ends at 10 p.m. Yours truly, on the other hand, usually leaves early. I console myself by saying it's because I work during the day. Staring at a computer can really wipe you out physically.

Current guidelines for minimum exercise are 30 minutes of moderate physical activity in "bursts of no less than 10 minutes each." I get that last part by walking Ruffy, my husband's dog. Every 10 minutes, Ruffy tries to burst from his leash, thereby bursting my arm out of its socket.

~ Comments ~

Chapter 13c

Anita: "Seniors have the same complaints about exercise as do their younger counterparts:

It's boring. It hurts.
They're too busy.
Their horoscope warned them against it. They inherited a flawed gene from an ancestor who dropped dead while exercising on the deck of the *Mayflower.*"

~~

For a February 1991 issue of *The Weekly Vista*, Anita wrote an **award-winning column** thanking Suzanne Somers. An excerpt follows:

"Don't you just adore that commercial with **Suzanne Somers**? I sure do. Think of it. Millions of us women out here are needlessly suffering from cellulite hips and gelatinous thighs when all we need do is spend $29.95 plus shipping and handling for a contraption that looks like something made by slave labor in Bucharest.

"Forget all those aerobics you've been doing. Throw away that Nordic Track. Say goodbye to bicycling, walking, or whatever your choice of poison to reduce those thunder-thighs. Just order Somers' little product, and in no time you too can join the ranks of those pencil-thighed, grinning mooncalves seen in that commercial. Thanks, Thighmaster."

~~

Q. Anita, how do you really feel about exercise?
"I love dancing, hate exercising."

~~

I call Ruffy "my husband's dog," because he (the dog) was there before I moved in. Ruffy was not happy to see me, and the feeling was mutual. He growled, snarled and strained at his leash every time I came into sight. "Good doggy. Nice doggy. Hope you drop dead, doggy," said brave little me.

I finally won Ruffy over with leftovers, soft words and threatening to clobber him if he didn't shut the heck up.

Did you know that hefting a five-pound pipe over your head is good exercise? ★

A Missed Opportunity

ARKANSAS WRITERS' CONFERENCE
June 2-5, 1999
Jean Strong, Wit and Wisdom Award, 1ˢᵗ

IT was the noon hour in New York City on a sunny spring day early in the 1960s. I was walking north on Broadway, returning to my office in Rockefeller Center after purchasing tickets for a play that a friend and I planned to attend.

My trim five-feet-eight, 35-year-old frame was sheathed in a stylish gray suit. Heels and hose completed this workaday costume. The suit did not conceal my well-rounded contours. In the mix of New Yorkers and visitors moving along the Manhattan street, I looked the part of a well-dressed worker in the publishing field.

Suddenly a suited man in his mid-forties fell into step beside me. By New York standards he appeared somewhat seedy, but he had a pleasant face. He introduced himself. He was from Kentucky and he would like to recruit me as a lady wrestler. It pays well, he explained. "I think you would do well at it."

I smiled to myself. As a newspaper photographer-writer, I had met a lady wrestler named Gorgeous Georgia. She was an attractive person, with long brunette hair and a figure not unlike my own.

In my youth on an Iowa farm I had milked cows, tended horses, helped my father with fieldwork—and dreamed of traveling. I had not considered the potential for travel as a lady wrestler.

As I recall, the man from Kentucky mentioned a $250 weekly salary—a bit more than I was earning as a reporter-researcher for *Fortune*, the business magazine.

I could not be offended by this man who had singled me out, among Manhattan's millions, as a worthy candidate for the bogus art. But I doubted my ability to passionately pursue such a career.

Still, a civil offer, though spontaneous and startling, requires a civil reply. "I already have a good job. But thank you just the same," said I.

Thinking back and reflecting on my long journalistic career in New York and elsewhere, I view this as one of several

~ Comments ~

"Contests provide incentive for writers to practice and hone their skills. And winning can be such a delightful surprise."
—Jean Strong

Chapter 13d

Jean: "For my memoirs, I plan a chapter on 'missed opportunities.' Of course, opportunities are never lost; someone will take the ones we miss.

"This 1960s incident came to mind when I read the contest rules for the 1999 Arkansas Writers' Conference. They specified a maximum word count and said each 'wit and wisdom' entry should be titled, 'If I Woulda . . .'
~~
New York City is a great place. If you live in mid-town Manhattan you can walk to work, to Saks' 5ᵗʰ Avenue and to pick up theater tickets. After eight years I no longer wanted to compete for a space to walk in, sit in or just be.

Later in **Philadelphia** I lived in a high-rise apartment overlooking Washington Square and the Liberty Bell and walked one block to work at *Farm Journal*. Living was less stressful but the job provided more than enough stress.

In **Bentonville, Arkansas** I live in a ground-floor apartment six blocks from the downtown square. I can walk to my bank, to the grocery and to several eating places, getting needed exercise while going about daily living.

Parking can be challenging or convenient, depending on the city. In **New York** my garage was a 45-block subway ride from my apartment.

Philadelphia was not auto-friendly and I rented a car when I wanted to go out-of-town.

In **DC** I parked on the street close by my ground-floor apartment on Wisconsin Avenue near Washington Cathedral. I rode the bus downtown and to work on missed opportunities. If I had said 'yes,' I might have become a contender as Marlon Brando failed to do in "On the Waterfront."

If I had engaged in more physical activity, I might not now be carrying as many extra pounds—and I might have been elected a state governor.

But come to think of it, had I succumbed to his offer I might not be as happy as I am today—a retired journalist entering contests, writing articles for magazines, working on my memoirs—free of worry about earning enough to pay the rent.

Writing in retirement can be rewarding and fun. My career as a lady wrestler would have been brief, and the medical benefits less bountiful than those provided by Time, Inc. (now AOL Time Warner).

Women sports figures are forced into retirement before age 50 when a journalist's life is just getting more interesting. ★

~ Comments ~

Chapter 13d continued

The Hill where parking was scarce. Later and for seven and one-half years I drove to Time-Life Books and parked on the street in Alexandria, Virginia.

In **Bentonville** I have an attached garage with an automatic door opener, a convenience greatly appreciated. I walk to places within half a mile and drive to our post office (new in 2001) that is two miles from my home. Parking isn't a problem as I roam around the entire area to shop, eat and play although traffic has increased greatly in the past 10 years.

While density of population does mean more efficient **land use** than we have in NW Arkansas, it also means more stressful living conditions. A news story in the *Morning News* (3/31/02) points out the differences between towns and cities in Northwest Arkansas, based on newly released 2000 census figures.

The retirement village of **Bella Vista** (population 16,582) takes up 65.58 square miles of land space while **Fayetteville** (58,047 population) encompasses 43.43 square miles. That means population density per square mile is 252.8 persons in Bella Vista, and 1,336.6 in the university town of Fayetteville.

Springdale (45,798) has a population density of 1,463 per sq. mi. in its 31.3 square mile area.

Rogers (38,829) 33.53 square miles, has 1,158 population density.

Bentonville (19,730) occupies 21.24 square miles with 928.9 density.

NW Arkansas is a better retirement area for me than Manhattan or DC.

~~

14. HELPING HANDS

Guidelines and Tips for Writers
VOICES FROM THE MID-SOUTH, COPYRIGHT © 2002

I F you are reading this book from the back, last chapter first, you are probably interested in planning and writing a newspaper column of your own, or writing Letters to the Editor of your local newspaper. We offer guidelines to help. You will find a student subject notebook of lined paper helpful, along with a few pens or pencils.

Subject matter. Generally, you should write about what you know or can learn about through research. Our columns—and the Contents page listing them by category and headline—may suggest topics and column ideas to you.

Anita suggests: *"For human-interest columns, write about experiences and feelings that are common to us all."*

Daily Record editor Kent Marts told us, "The best material for community newspaper columns generally isn't a weighty national subject; rather, the best material covers matters that are often close to the hearts of the writers."

Executive editor Jim Morriss, *Morning News*, says that "topics abound." He adds, "The region is in transition, with a metropolitan lifestyle evolving from a totally rural environment, and the ongoing efforts to achieve a balance between the two is fertile ground for reporting and commentary."

Style. You can analyze the diverse styles of the three VOICES' writers, but you will develop a style of your own. Style emanates from the individual. Study columns you like in your newspapers. As you share your views and observances in letters to editors or "letters to readers," your own style will emerge.

Objective. A column can provoke, intrigue, inform, or amuse. It represents a friendly handshake between columnist and reader who might be enjoying a cup of coffee or tea at the time of reading.

~ Comments ~

Chapter 14

"Northwest Arkansas continues to offer **opportunities for future columnists** who by the way must pay their dues as reporters before assuming the columnist mantle with any of the local newspapers. Topics abound. The region is in transition, with a metropolitan lifestyle evolving from a totally rural environment, and the ongoing efforts to achieve a balance between the two is fertile ground for reporting and commentary.

"For aspiring writers/journalists, the University of Arkansas has both a strong creative writing program and an aggressive journalism department that focuses on producing trained, knowledgeable reporters."
—Jim Morriss, executive editor Morning News.

~~

"**Newspapers thrive** on keeping the voices of staff out of news stories. Personal opinions, editorial comments, insights are all forbidden in most areas of newspapers. But, often buried on inside pages, the rules change: Staff members (and often community members) are given a few inches in which to write whatever they please. They get to write a column.

"Very often, when we say columnists, we think of national commentary on weighty, important subjects which impact everyone; yet for community newspapers, that is often not the case. The columns touch on apparently insignificant issues, but that doesn't mean the writers don't touch people's lives."
— Kent Marks, Editor, Daily Record.

~~

"Sportswriter Red Smith once wrote: 'Writing is easy. I just open a vein and bleed.'"
—Anita's e-mail

A good column will create some reaction in the reader. Anita suggests: *"Your column should either make readers think, laugh, cry or get angry. Just don't make them yawn."*

Columnists enjoy hearing reader's reaction to a column. Feedback is rewarding. Check your facts, be accurate and avoid criticism for careless mistakes.

A political columnist we knew in Iowa [Frank Nye, *Cedar Rapids Gazette*] said he knew he must be doing a good job when members of both political parties berated him for his partisanship—in the same column.

So what kind of column can you best write? Human interest (like Anita's) or topics to serve the interests of a target audience (like Cynthia's EQUINOTES or Jean's TEEN TALK)? List things that inspire or excite you, and examine the list for possible topics.

You Can Write a Column by Monica McCabe Cardoza (Writer's Digest, 2000) would be a useful companion volume to the book you hold in your hand. While their 'how to' book does not include sample columns, it does offer useful information.

Cordoza's book is divided into three parts:
1. Before Beginning
2. Writing the Column, and
3. Selling the Column

Cardoza's perspective is for columnists who seek syndication and publication in as many newspapers as possible. You may find the advice in Parts 1 and 2 useful for writing a local newspaper column.

<u>Warming up exercises</u>

You can proceed at your own speed with the following exercises:

#1. In your notebook or sheet of lined paper, write: **"I like or am passionate about . . ."**

Cynthia suggests: *"List 25 things and explain why you like each, and why others should like it."* This will help you determine whether it might be of interest to others.
a. Topic
b. Why I like the topic
c. Why others should like this topic.

#2. Study the Contents page of this book; **list the subjects** that suggest column ideas for you.

Chapter 14 continued

These references are often found in the libraries of writers who want to improve their writing skills:

The Elements of Style, William Strunk Jr. and E. B. White. Macmillan, 1979 – 1999.

On Writing Well, William Zinsser, 4th edition 1990, or Harper 2001. The classic guide to writing nonfiction that also gets republished periodically.

Sleeping Dogs Don't Lay, Practical Advice for the Grammatically Challenged, Richard Lederer and Richard Dowis. St. Marten's Press, 1999, 2001.

Check your library or bookstore for books with collected works by your favorites. Among them are some you might want to read.

Syndicated Columnists
Russell Baker
Dave Barry
Erma Bombeck
Jimmy Breslin
Art Buchwald
Herb Caen
Molly Ivins
Ellen Goodman
Bob Greene
Pete Kurth
John Lardner
Marya Mannes
Ernie Pyle
Ayn Rand
Mike Royko
Eleanor Roosevelt
H. Allen Smith
Red Smith
William Allen White
George Will
~~

#3. Study each of the columns in VOICES FROM THE MID-SOUTH and **list** what you believe are:

a. The **10 best leads.**
b. The **10 best middles.**
c. The **10 best endings.**

#4. **Write what you like best** about each of the 10 openings, middles and endings. Then jot down the shortcomings you perceive. There are no right or wrong answers; we want <u>you</u> to write winning openings, closings and middles. Recognizing good examples and not-so-good examples will improve your own efforts. In studying and analyzing these columns and others you find in your local newspapers and elsewhere, you will learn what makes compelling reading for you. Ask yourself: Will the newspaper audience I want to write for like my subject matter?

Summarize your observations to **create personal guidelines** as aids to your own work.

I like as best leads. . .
I like as best middles. . .
I like as best endings. . .
And for each list
   a. Shortcomings
   b. Strengths

#5. "Read other authors' work," says Anita. *"I firmly believe that a good columnist or any writer must also be an avid reader. You don't have to copy their style, but you will almost by osmosis pick up on what and what not to do."*

Creating Your Columns

A. From your No. 1 list above, **select one of the subjects. Write a headline** to give yourself a goal or objective. [Headlines also give the editor a quick idea of what the column is about. Editors might not use your headline, but it serves a useful purpose in pinpointing the gist of the column.] Some writers like to write the column first and then the headline.

B. **Outline or list the information** you will include **in the body** of your column:

   a. The lead paragraph (attention grabber)
   b. The middle (points to be made)
   c. Craft your ending (now or later)
   d. **List possible endings.** You can craft your exit line(s) with flourish and style.

~ Comments ~

Chapter 14 continued

> "That the media have public responsibility so important that it is protected by the Constitution gets lost in the profit chase. Our leaders may have other sources of information—though the intelligence community has not covered itself with glory—but they, too, are influenced by the daily media blat. No wonder we were asleep at the wheel."
> —Molly Ivins, November 2001

Another Balloon Story
A man in a hot air balloon realized he was lost. Reducing altitude he spotted a woman below, and descended a bit more to within shouting distance.

"Excuse me, can you help me? I promised a friend I would meet him an hour ago, but I don't know where I am!"

"You are in a hot air balloon approximately 30 feet above the ground. You are between 40 and 41 degrees north latitude and between 59 and 60 degrees west longitude.

"You must be a Republican," said the balloonist.

"I am. How did you know?"

"Well, everything you told me sounds technically correct, but I have no idea what to make of your information, and the fact is, I am still lost. You have not been much help so far."

"You must be a Democrat," replied the woman.

"I am, but how did you know?"

"Well, you don't know where you are or where you are going. You have risen to where you are due to a large quantity of hot air. You made a promise that you have no idea how to keep, and expect

C. Draft your column.
   a. Does the beginning entice the reader?
   b. Does the middle provide a satisfying body of information, logic or nonsense?
   c. Does the column end with a bang, provoke a chuckle or other reaction?

D. Repeat steps A through C above.
   You will need a half dozen or more samples to convince an editor that you can write and sustain a column.

Rewriting is part of the process—to make it the best you can. As you become proficient, you may get by with three or four rewrites. Few, if any writers, produce an acceptable column with the first draft.

Anita says: *"No matter how many times you rewrite it— and you should—you can read it months or even weeks later and see how you could have said it better."*

Sounds like work? Yes, it is. But there is also satisfaction in a job well done. And some of us are born to love writing or, as some will tell you, they love 'having written.'

<u>Name your column</u>
   Every person and every column deserves a name. **Brainstorm titles for your column.** Write your title ideas in your notebook or on a lined sheet of paper for further study. Refer to it a week or so later and add more titles or choose from among those you have already noted. The title you choose is your new friend, and constant companion, a challenge to observe and write for the edification and amusement of others. They will become — YOUR AUDIENCE.

Make it a habit to write something each and every day while you master the art of writing a successful newspaper column or letter to the editor.

And, of course, we recommend especially that you read and enjoy the columns in this book that were written by Anita French Creech and Cynthia Haseloff.

Good luck! ★

~ Comments ~

"I look at myself and wonder why I ever thought a column could exist under my dominion. Well, I have loved writing and it is a habit hard to break. If enough of you will write a card and say 'quit' it might work."
—Roberta Fulbright, 1947

<u>Chapter 14 continued</u>

me to solve your problem. The fact is you are in exactly the same position you were in before we met, but somehow it's my fault."
  —Jean's e-mail

~~

One must above all things be careful to pass muster at the bar of his own judgment rather than that of others."
—Roberta Fulbright, quoting Confucius, in her last column 21 May 1952.

For Your Notes

For Your Notes

Anita French Creech   Cynthia Haseloff   Jean Strong

VOICES FROM THE MID SOUTH is not a chorus of southern voices. Only one of the three writers is southern-born; the other two came to beautiful Northwest Arkansas from California and Iowa. The book's charm lies in its sharing of diverse experiences, memories and career information as revealed in newspaper columns and comments by a western novelist, a mother-turned-journalist in mid-life and a career journalist, now retired. The final chapter offers tips, guidelines and encouragement for aspiring writers.

READERS COMMENTS

"**VOICES FROM THE MID-SOUTH** showcases the talents of women newspaper columnists and provides a kaleidoscope of wit, wisdom and warmth. The reader who picks it up will get a pickup of pleasure from its observations of life and living."
—**Nan Snow and Dorothy Stuck**, authors, Little Rock

"**Northwest Arkansas** has helped nurture the careers of these columnists. The virtual orgy of growth during the decade of the '90s produced a newspaper competition which provided more writing opportunities that in turn led to the quest for new topics and people of interest. The ability to mine those new sources of interest and convert them into reflections of the region's personality marks them as columnists vs. standard newspaper reporting.

"The region continues to offer opportunities for future columnists who, by the way, must pay their dues as reporters before assuming the columnist mantle with any of the local newspapers. Topics abound. The region is in transition, with a metropolitan lifestyle evolving from a totally rural environment, and the ongoing efforts to achieve a balance between the two is fertile ground for reporting and commentary.

"For aspiring writers/journalists, the University of Arkansas has both a strong creative writing program and an aggressive journalism department that focuses on producing trained, knowledgeable reporters."
—**Jim Morriss**, *Morning News* executive editor, Springdale

"**Newspapers thrive** on keeping the voices of staff out of news stories. Personal opinions, editorial comments, insights are all forbidden in most areas of newspapers. But, often buried on inside pages, the rules change: Staff members (and often community members) are given a few inches in which to write whatever they please. They get to write a column.

Very often when we say columnists we think of national commentary on weighty, important subjects which impact everyone; yet for community newspapers, that is often not the case. The columns touch on apparently insignificant issues, but that doesn't mean the writers don't touch people's lives.

"Years ago, I wrote a column about the monarch butterfly migration through Benton County. I was suffering from writer's block while trying to write my weekly column;

(READERS COMMENTS continued next page)

nothing came to mind but those butterflies. So I wrote about them. The day the column was published, the phone started ringing and people stopped me to talk about it. The response over those 750-or-so words was overwhelming. All over butterflies.

"It turns out that the best material for community newspaper columns generally isn't a weighty national subject; rather, the best material covers matters that are often close to the hearts of the writers. With titles such as "It's My Pity Party," "How the Café Was Named," "A Day at the Flea Markets" and "Good Fences Make Good Neighbors." I'm sure you'll find these writers are speaking from their hearts.
—**Kent Marts**, *Benton County Daily Record* editor, Bentonville

"**I did enjoy** the articles and comments. All of the writers have a tremendous sense of humor which is in short supply in larger newspapers. My concern is the format with the column and comments running side by side. I find this difficult to read because one has to read one column all the way through and then go back and read through the other. I wish you success with the book and I would love to have a book signing."
—**Ann Luer**, owner Faybles Bookstore, Fayetteville

"**This is a collection** of most informative and readable newspaper columns. What makes this collection particularly important is that the reader gets to know and understand the writers through accompanying commentary. This is a very enjoyable book."
—**Bob Besom**, Director, Shiloh Museum of Ozark History, Springdale

"**Your idea** of combining three people's columns plus the use of side-bar comments is unique and ties together all five women. The presence of Fulbright and Duncan is felt throughout the book.

"There is a crispness and newness to each chapter—you feel and recognize the individual personality of each writer, yet there is a sameness of character and breeding—the independent drive and basic understanding of the human psyche.

"You have put together a 'good thing'—the writing hints at the end are a marvelous teaching tool for creative writing instructors or for just 'wannabees' like me."
—**Myra Moran**, specialist in Arkansas books, Rogers

A Very Special Gift
for family,
friends
or
newcomers

You can purchase
VOICES FROM THE MID-SOUTH
At your local bookstore
or from the publisher:

PRAIRIE ALMANAC PUBLISHER
PO Box 1312, Dept. V
Bentonville, AR 72712-1312

Phone: 479-271-8459
E-mail: PA Publisher@aol.com

Prices for these Publisher Specials
include postage & handling:

VOICES from the Mid-South
$16.95

A PRAIRIE ALMANAC
1839 TO 1919,
the eyewitness story about
everyday life of pioneers
$14.95

ORDER FORM
Dear PA Publisher:
    PO Box 1312-V, Bentonville, AR 72712-1312
Enclosed please find check / money order in
the amount of $_____ for
#

___ *VOICES from the Mid-South*, **$16.95**

___ *A Prairie Almanac*, **$14.95**

___ **Both books for $24.50 [save $7.40]**

Send book(s) to:

Name_____

_____

_____
City   State   Zip

Mail your order to:
PA Publisher
PO Box 1312, Dept. V
Bentonville, AR 72712-1312

ORDER FORM
Dear PA Publisher:
    PO Box 1312-V, Bentonville, AR 72712-1312
Enclosed please find check / money order in
the amount of $_____ for
#

___ *VOICES from the Mid-South*, **$16.95**

___ *A Prairie Almanac*, **$14.95**

___ **both books for $24.50 [save $7.40]**

Send book(s) to:

Name_____

_____

_____
City   State   Zip